THE REED FIELD GUIDE TO
NEW ZEALAND
NATIVE TREES

THE REED FIELD GUIDE TO
NEW ZEALAND
NATIVE TREES

J.T. Salmon

C.B.E., D.Sc., F.R.S.N.Z., F.R.P.S.,
Professor Emeritus,
Victoria University of Wellington

REED

The Author

John Salmon, a Professor Emeritus of Victoria University of Wellington, has become well known to the New Zealand public with the publication of his successful *The Native Trees of New Zealand.*

Profesor Salmon was educated at Wellington College and Victoria University of Wellington. All his life he has travelled about New Zealand, enjoying the wilderness and out-of-the-way places. He is well known as a nature photographer, as a writer and broadcaster on scientific subjects, and as a lecturer. His book *Heritage Destroyed*, published in 1960, helped to arouse a national awakening to the importance of nature conservation. *The Native Trees of New Zealand* (1980) and *Native New Zealand Flowering Plants* (1991) have proved to be among our most popular books on native plants. The author is a Fellow of both the Royal Society of New Zealand and the Royal Photographic Society.

The father of four sons, Professor Salmon now lives in retirement at Taupo with his wife Pam.

Published by Reed Books, a division of Reed Publishing (NZ) Ltd, 39 Rawene Road, Birkenhead, Auckland. Associated companies, branches and representatives throughout the world.

ISBN 0 7900 0381 3

First published 1986
Reprinted 1990, 1991, 1994

Printed in Singapore

To my wife Pam

Acknowledgements

This small book was envisaged by the publishers of *The Native Trees of New Zealand* as a corollary to the publication of that book. It has been produced directly from *The Native Trees of New Zealand* by condensation and cropping of both the plates and the text. As the source material remains the same as for the larger book there is little need for further lengthy acknowledgements.

The publication of this field guide marks the conclusion of a project that has extended over the past twenty-two years and it is fitting now that I acknowledge the great help I received from my wife Pam over all those years. Her unstinted support, useful criticisms, proofreading and, above all, her company and help in searching for specimens to photograph in out-of-the-way places has been tremendous. The fine specimen of *Urostemon kirkii* which appears in the picture on page 6 of *The Native Trees* was one of her great finds.

Introduction

In my publisher's original concept, this field guide was seen as a guide to the common trees. However, the word common has different connotations depending on where, in New Zealand's forests, you happen to be looking at any particular time. Trees that are common in one place are uncommon elsewhere and vice versa. In discussing this with friends and colleagues it soon became clear that a field guide that was complete, or as near complete as possible, would be preferable.

In compiling this field guide from the material in *The Native Trees of New Zealand* I decided that most people would be interested primarily in those trees they find on the three main islands of New Zealand. The first step, therefore, was to eliminate all species from the outlying islands of the New Zealand region and confine the guide to the North, South and Stewart Islands. To conserve space the tree ferns also have been omitted. As the book is a guide only, drastic condensation of both the pictures and the text from the original book was necessary. By restricting plates to the bare necessities along with frequent cropping of the originals and a much-reduced text, a field guide has been produced which covers all the native trees found on the three main islands of New Zealand. This complete guide should fill a long-felt need. I would refer those seeking further information on our New Zealand trees to my larger book *The Native Trees of New Zealand* and to the further works listed in its bibliography.

J. T. Salmon
Taupo, January 1985

Identifying New Zealand Trees

Any guide to living things must, as its name implies, be brief and follow some classification system. The system used in this field guide follows that in the original book which was based on *Flora of New Zealand*. (Vol 1, 1961, by H. H. Allan and Vol. 2, 1970, by L B. Moore and E. Edgar.) Common names and the Maori names for our trees, wherever these exist, are included with the botanical names. As in my larger book, Allan's classification and nomenclatural priorities have been departed from in some places to achieve acceptable page design, but, except for matagouri (*Discaria toumatou*), such changes are minor.

Trees grow and disappear through ageing, climatic accidents and the march of so-called human progress which destroys many of them. The dates given with captions of tree pictures will be useful from this historical aspect while those given with flower and fruit pictures indicate the time of year the photograph was taken and hence the flowering and fruiting times of each species.

The botanical enthusiast can follow the classification system in seeking identifications while novices may find it easier to match up their specimens with the pictures by searching through the book. In the case of the tall forest trees, bark pictures are included as these trees can be identified from bark when leaves and flowers are out of reach. Illustrations of each species have been included in most cases, but amongst genera of similar trees such as *Coprosma, Olearia* and *Dracophyllum* the number of whole-tree illustrations has been reduced. To assist with identification, the illustrations of leaves, flowers and fruits have been reproduced at about natural size whenever possible, or else the degree of magnification is given.

During the last few years systematic revisions of various sections of our native flora have resulted in some changes of hitherto familiar names. For this reason the reader may encounter discrepancies between the names used in this book and those appearing in the first edition of *The Native Trees of New Zealand*. The 1986 revised edition includes all these name changes.

The species

This part provides a guide to species contained in *The Reed Field Guide to New Zealand Native Trees.* Although a general index and an index of common names can be found at the end of the book, this table will enable the reader to locate each tree species quickly.

Kahikatea/White pine *Dacrycarpus dacrydioides*

Reaching to 60 m, this is the tallest New Zealand tree. It is found all over the country from sea level to 600 m particularly in swampy areas, although it grows quite well on dry sites and hillsides.

2

Fig 1 A mature kahikatea near Ross, Westland, 1971.

Fig 2 The flakey bark of kahikatea.

Fig 3 Juvenile foliage differs from adult foliage by having the leaves arising as two rows along the stems. (x2)

Fig 4 Male cones with mature foliage of scale-like leaves, each up to 2 mm long, appressed to the branchlets. (approx x1)

Fig 5 Ripe seeds on their red receptacles, April. (approx x1)

Family *Podocarpaceae*
Genus *Dacrycarpus*

4

5

3

Matai/Black pine *Prumnopitys taxifolia*

1

A robust forest tree up to 25 m high with a trunk up to 1.3 m through, found throughout New Zealand.

2

3

Fig 1 A mature matai at Woodside Gorge, 1973.

Fig 2 Ripe male cones, November. (approx x1)

Fig 3 A ripe matai seed with its typical purplish bloom, February. (approx x1)

Fig 4 Bark of an old matai showing typical flaking.

Fig 5 A juvenile matai at the shrub stage.

Family *Podocarpaceae*
Genus *Prumnopitys*

4

5

Miro/Brown pine *Prumnopitys ferruginea*

A tall, round-headed, forest tree up to 25 m high with a trunk up to 1 m across. Found all over New Zealand in lowland forests from sea level to 1,000 m.

2　3

4

Fig 1 A fine specimen of miro, Opepe Bush, 1965.

Fig 2 Miro bark showing the typical pitted surface and scaling.

Fig 3 A cluster of ripe miro seeds, November. (slightly enlarged)

Fig 4 Male cones stand erect from the branchlets to release their pollen, October.

Totara *Podocarpus totara* and **montane totara** *P. cunninghamii*

Fig 1 The Pouakani totara near Mangapehi, 1979.

1

12

2

3

Both totaras are found in forests throughout New Zealand. Totara grows to 30 m high with a trunk 2 m across and montane totara (formerly Hall's totara) reaches 20 m with a trunk 1.25 m across. A third species growing to 9 m high, *P. lawrencii*, is found from Marlborough to south Westland and has pungent, needle-sharp leaves 1.5–2.5 cm long by 1–3.5 mm wide.

Fig 2 The bark of montane totara is thin and papery.

Fig 3 The bark of totara is thick, stringy and furrowed.

Fig 4 Ripe totara seeds in their receptacles, April. (approx x1)

Fig 5 A montane totara tree growing near Moawhango, 1969.

Family *Podocarpaceae*
Genus *Podocarpus*

5

4

Bog pine/Mountain pine *Halocarpus bidwillii*

1

Bog pine usually grows as a spreading or erect, closely-branching shrub, but occasionally as a small tree up to 3.5 m high. Horizontal branches may root as they grow outwards. It grows on dry stoney ground or in bogs between about 600 and 1,500 m altitude from Cape Colville south to Stewart Island.

2

3

Fig 1 A huge spreading bog pine plant near Te Anau, 1975.

Fig 2 A spray showing thick juvenile leaves at top with, lower down, the scale-like appressed adult leaves. (x3)

Fig 3 Ripe male cones, November. (x3)

Fig 4 Ripe seeds, March. (x2)

Fig 5 Branchlets showing the scale-like adult leaves. (x4)

Family *Podocarpaceae*
Genus *Halocarpus*

4

5

Yellow pine   *Halocarpus biformis*

In forest yellow pine forms a small tree reaching 10 m high but in exposed places it forms a tight, cypress-like bush perhaps only 1 m high. It occurs from sea level to 1,400 m from the Volcanic Plateau south to Stewart Island.

Fig 1 A spray with juvenile leaves passing to adult leaves below.

Fig 2 The strongly keeled, appressed adult leaves have translucent margins and conspicuous stomata. (x4)

Fig 3 Female cones occur singly or as twins and triplets, February. (x8)

Fig 4 Male cones are short, 2–5 mm long, January. (x5)

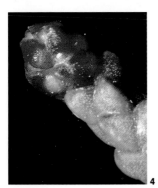

Yellow silver pine *Lepidothamnus intermedius*

A small, spreading tree up to 15 m high, of scattered occurrence in North Island forests but more common on the South Island's west coast and swampy forests of Stewart Island from sea level to 900 m.

Fig 1 A branchlet with adult leaves at the tip passing down to semi-adult leaves and juvenile leaves below. (approx x1)

Fig 2 Branchlet with semi-adult and adult leaves; both are keeled and have several irregular rows of stomata. (x2)

Fig 3 A ripe male cone, November. (x10)

Fig 4 A ripe female cone, April. (x10)

Fig 5 The bark is finely pitted, mottled and does not readily peel.

Family *Podocarpaceae*   Genus *Lepidothamnus*

Silver pine *Lagarostrobos colensoi*

Fig 1 A fine specimen growing on Mt Ruapehu, 1972.

2

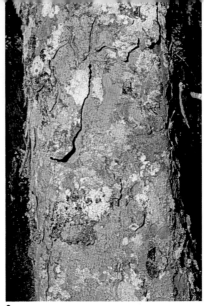

3

Silver pine is cone-shaped when young but grows to 15 m high with a canopy and a straight trunk 1 m through. It is found in forests from sea level to 950 m from Mangonui to Mt Ruapehu and along the west coast of the South Island mostly in shady situations.

Fig 2 The longitudinal ridging and pimpling typical of the bark of a young tree.

Fig 3 Typical bark of a mature tree.

Fig 4 The ripe male cone, October. (x4)

Fig 5 A ripe female cone, April. (x4)

Fig 6 Adult leaves, up to 2.5 mm long, have subacute tips and sparse, irregularly arranged stomata. (x4)

Family *Podocarpaceae*
Genus *Lagarostrobos*

6

4

5

Rimu/Red pine

Dacrydium cupressinum

A forest tree reaching 20–35 m high, occasionally higher, with a trunk up to 1.5 m through and sometimes even thicker. With its pendulous foliage rimu is a graceful and beautiful tree at all stages of growth.

Fig 1 A fine rimu growing at Opepe Bush, 1973.

Fig 2 The trunk and bark of a large rimu at Opepe Bush, 1965.

Fig 3 Male cones with adult foliage, November. (approx x1)

Fig 4 Adult foliage and ripe seeds on their red receptacles, April. (x4)

Family *Podocarpaceae*
Genus *Dacrydium*

Monoao   *Halocarpus kirkii*

3

5

4

6

A handsome tree not unlike a kauri when seen from a distance. Grows to a height of 25 m with a trunk 1 m through. It occurs sporadically in lowland forests between sea level and 700 m from Hokianga Harbour south to the Coromandel Peninsula.

Fig 1 Fine specimens of monoao trees, Kauaeranga Valley, 1971.

Fig 2 The thick, flaking, pustular bark of monoao.

Fig 3 Juvenile leaves. These may persist on trees up to 10 m high (x1)

Fig 4 The thick leathery adult leaves have faint keels, translucent margins and many irregularly arranged stomata. (x3)

Fig 5 A ripe female cone, April. (x4)

Fig 6 A ripe male cone, December. (x4)

Tanekaha/Celery pine *Phyllocladus trichomanoides*

1

2   **3**

A tall, pyramidal tree up to 20 m high found in lowland forests between sea level and 800 m from North Cape south to Wanganui and Waipukurau.

Fig 1 A tanekaha growing in the Kauaeranga Valley, 1974.

Fig 2 The bark of a young tanekaha.

Fig 3 The bark of a mature tanekaha.

Fig 4 Male cones at the tip of a rachide (branchlet) surrounded by a whorl of phylloclads, October. (x1.5)

Fig 5 Whorls of rachides bearing phylloclads and female cones, the outer ones being about nine months old, October. (approx x1)

Family *Podocarpaceae*
Genus *Phyllocladus*

4   **5**

Toatoa   *Phyllocladus glaucus*
and **mountain toatoa**   *P. aspleniifolius* var.   *alpinus*

Fig 1 Mountain toatoa growing on the Volcanic Plateau, 1973.

Fig 2 A phylloclad of mountain toatoa. (x2)

Fig 3 Phylloclads of toatoa with female cones along the rachides. (x0.5)

Fig 4 Male cones of toatoa, December. (approx x1)

1

3

26

5

6

Toatoa grows up to 15 m high and is found in lowland forests from Mangonui south to Rotorua. Mountain toatoa reaches up to 9 m high and is found between 900 and 1,600 m altitude from Coromandel south in the North Island while in the South Island it grows near sea level in Southland and south Westland.

Fig 5 The bark of mountain toatoa; toatoa bark is similar but coarser.

Fig 6 Male cones of mountain toatoa, December. (x10)

Fig 7 Mature female cones of toatoa, July. (x2)

Fig 8 Female cones of mountain toatoa with ripe seeds, February. (x8)

7

8

27

Kawaka *Libocedrus plumosa* and **pahautea** *L. bidwillii*

The New Zealand cedars. Kawaka reaches 25 m in height, pahautea 20 m. Kawaka occurs in the north from sea level to 600 m between Mangonui and Rotorua while in the south it is found in north-west Nelson. Pahautea occurs between 250 and 1,200 m from Mt Te Aroha south and is common at lower levels on the west coast of the South Island.

2   **3**

Fig 1 A group of pahautea trees in Hihitahi State Forest, April 1969.

Fig 2 Pahautea foliage. (x2)

Fig 3 Kawaka foliage. (x2)

Fig 4 Male cones of pahautea; kawaka cones are similar. (x1.5)

Fig 5 A mature pahautea female cone; kawaka cones are similar. (x3)

Fig 6 Pahautea bark; kawaka bark is similar.

Family *Cupressaceae*
Genus *Libocedrus*

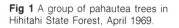

5   **6**

Kauri *Agathis australis*

A massive tree, up to 30 m high with a trunk 3 m through, bearing a huge spreading crown on immense swollen branches. Found from Northland south to about Tauranga.

2

3

Fig 1 Known as the McKinley Kauri, this fine tree grows in Parry Park near Warkworth. Photographed in December 1977.

Fig 2 Kauri bark.

Fig 3 Male cone. (approx x1)

Fig 4 Mature female cones. (x0.5)

Fig 5 Young kauri leaves. (x0.5)

Family *Araucariaceae*
Genus *Agathis*

4

5

31

Tawa *Beilschmiedia tawa*

1

2

A tall forest tree with a spreading crown, reaching 25 m high with a trunk 1.2 m through. Found throughout northern New Zealand, south to the Clarence River and Westport.

32

3

4

5

Fig 1 A fine tawa growing near Barryville, May 1972.

Fig 2 The bark of tawa.

Fig 3 Young foliage of tawa with flower buds. (x0.5)

Fig 4 Flower panicles of tawa. (x0.5)

Fig 5 Tawa drupes, Waikanae, March 1978. (x2)

Family *Lauraceae*
Genus *Beilschmiedia*

33

Taraire *Beilschmiedia tarairi*

A tall forest tree up to 22 m high with a straight trunk 1 m through and distinctive leaves. Found from North Cape to Raglan and Mt Hikurangi.

34

4

Fig 1 A typical taraire from near Kerikeri, February 1965.

Fig 2 A typical leaf, upper surface.(x0.5)

Fig 3 A spray of flowers, Whangarei, December 1970. (x0.5)

Fig 4 Taraire drupes, Auckland, May 1961. (x0.5)

Fig 5 The thick, velvety tomentum that clothes the stalks and leaf veins. (x1)

Fig 6 The bark of taraire.

6

Pigeonwood/Porokaiwhiri _Hedycarya arborea_

Fig 1

A small, aromatic, erect tree up to 12 m high with thick, leathery leaves. Found in wet areas with rich soils throughout the North Island and south to Banks Peninsula.

Fig 2

Fig 1 A fine pigeonwood from Waiorongomai, March 1975.

Fig 2 Pigeonwood bark.

Fig 3 Ripening drupes, Lake Pounui, November 1968. (x0.5)

Fig 4 Male flowers, October. (x4)

Fig 5 Female flowers, December. (x4)

Fig 6 The faintly-grooved, pubescent branchlet. (x2)

Fig 7 A leaf undersurface. (x0.5)

Family _Monimiaceae_
Genus _Hedycarya_

3

6

4

5

7

Horopito *Pseudowintera colorata* and **pepper tree** *P. axillaris*

1

Small trees or shrubs reaching up to 10 m tall found throughout
most of New Zealand though pepper tree does not occur south of
Banks Peninsula and Westport.

Fig 1 A horopito tree, Mt Ruapehu,
March 1970.

Fig 2 The green, shining undersides of
pepper tree leaves. (x0.5)

Fig 3 A spray of pepper tree leaves.
(x0.5)

Fig 4 A flower and bud of horopito;
pepper tree has similar flowers. (x4)

Fig 5 The ripe berries are black in
horopito, orange-red in pepper tree. (x3)

Fig 6 Upper surface of a horopito leaf
showing typical red edging and
blotching. (x1)

Fig 7 Typical bluish undersurface of a
horopito leaf. (x1)

Family *Winteraceae*   Genus *Pseudowintera*

38

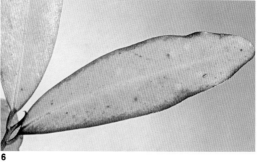

39

Mangeao *Litsea calicaris*

A small, much-branched tree up to 12 m high, erect in the forest but more rounded and spreading in the open. Found from North Cape south to Mokau and East Cape.

Fig 1 A fine mangeao growing near Hamurama Springs, March 1966.

Fig 2 Lower surface of leaf. (x0.5)

Fig 3 Bark of mangeao.

Fig 4 Flowers and foliage.

Fig 5 Opening flower bud, September. (x3)

Fig 6 Male flower shedding pollen, September. (x3)

Fig 7 Drupes, February. (x0.5)

Family *Lauraceae*
Genus *Litsea*

41

Pukatea *Laurelia novae-zelandiae*

A tall forest tree up to 36 m high with a prominently-buttressed
trunk 2 m through. Found in swampy areas throughout New Zealand
from sea level to 610 m.

2

3

6

4
5

Fig 1 A fine pukatea near Lake Rotoma, May 1972.

Fig 2 Male flowers with anthers but no stigma, October. (x1)

Fig 3 Female flower with staminodes and stigma but no stamens, November. (x4)

Fig 4 A bisexual flower with red stamens, yellow abortive staminodes and hairy styles with stigmas, November. (x4)

Fig 5 Seed cases splitting open to release the plumed fruits, March. (x1)

Fig 6 Pukatea leaves. (x0.5)

Family *Monimiaceae*
Genus *Laurelia*

43

Hutu   *Ascarina lucida*

A small aromatic tree up to 8 m high with red-coloured branchlets. Found from sea level to 760 m in forests, occasionally in the North Island but more commonly on the west coast of the South Island and on Stewart Island.

Fig 1 Hutu trees, Lake Matheson, 1973.

Fig 2 The leathery leaves of hutu are 2–8 cm long and up to 3.5 cm wide.

Fig 3 A spike of typical male flowers, September.

Family *Chloranthaceae*
Genus *Ascarina*

Kawakawa/Pepper tree
Macropiper excelsum

A small, densely-branched,
aromatic tree or shrub up to
6 m high, found from
Northland south to Banks
Peninsula and Okarito in
forests, shady gullies
and shaded rocky places.

Fig 1 A cluster of male spikes,
September. (x1)

Fig 2 The large, fleshy leaves are
up to 10 cm long by 12 cm wide.

Fig 3 A ripe female spike, February.
(x1)

Family *Piperaceae*
Genus *Macropiper*

Mahoe wao   *Melicytus lanceolatus*

A small, slender, erectly-branching tree up to 6 m high with a trunk up to 30 cm through. Found from sea level to 915 m in forests and along forest margins throughout New Zealand.

2

Fig 1 A typical mahoe wao tree with its distinctive white bark, West Taupo, December 1973.

Fig 2 Flowers clothe the branchlets in great profusion, September.

Fig 3 Mahoe wao bark.

Fig 4 A typical leaf. (approx x1)

Fig 5 Ripening berries become dark purple when fully ripe, April. (x1.5)

Family *Violaceae*
Genus *Melicytus*

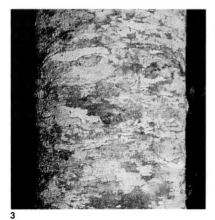

3

4

5

47

Mahoe/Whiteywood *Melicytus ramiflorus*
and **large-leaved whiteywood** *M. macrophyllus*

One of the commonest trees found throughout New Zealand in forests and scrublands, mahoe is a small, usually spreading tree up to 10 m high with a trunk up to 60 cm through. The large-leaved whiteywood is a small tree up to 6 m high found only from Northland south to the Waikato in forest from sea level to 600 m.

Fig 1 A typical mahoe tree, Poahau Valley, November 1970.

Fig 2 Underside of a large-leaved whiteywood leaf, which is longer and broader than a mahoe leaf. (x1)

Fig 3 A mahoe leaf. (approx x1)

Fig 4 Mahoe bark.

Fig 5 Ripe berries clothe the branchlets, March. (x1)

Fig 6 Male flowers, December. (x3)

Fig 7 Female flowers and new berries forming, November. (x1.5)

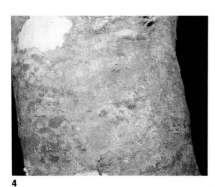

49

Kotukutuku/Native fuchsia *Fuchsia excorticata*

A small, usually spreading tree or shrub up to 14 m high, readily recognised by its peeling, red, papery outer bark. Kotukutuku is the largest fuchsia in the world and is found from sea level to 1,060 m throughout New Zealand in forests and scrublands.

2

4

Fig 1 A fine kotukutuku tree from Thundering Creek, Haast Pass, January 1973.

Fig 2 A leaf upper surface. (x1)

Fig 3 A leaf lower surface. (x1)

Fig 4 Kotukutuku flowers, November. (x0.5)

Fig 5 The trunk of a typical old tree.

Fig 6 Kotukutuku berries, January. (x2)

Family *Onagraceae*
Genus *Fuchsia*

5

6

3

1

Toru   *Toronia toru*

1

A much-branching, erect, small tree up to 12 m high, with the branches upwardly directed and a trunk about 20 cm through. Found from sea level to 850 m in forest and scrublands from Mangonui south to Tokomaru Bay.

2

3

Fig 1 A fine toru tree at Kaitoke, July 1973.

Fig 2 A raceme of flowers, November. (x0.5)

Fig 3 A branchlet showing dark upper and pale lower leaf surfaces and alternate leaves.

Fig 4 Toru drupes, April. (x1)

Fig 5 Toru bark.

Family *Proteaceae*
Genus *Toronia*

4

5

Rewarewa/New Zealand honeysuckle *Knightia excelsa*

1

2

A tall, upright, branching tree up to 40 m high with a trunk 1 m through. Found from sea level to 850 m throughout the North Island and in Marlborough in the South Island.

Fig 1 Rewarewa leaves. (x0.6)

Fig 2 A flower cluster or inflorescence of rewarewa, November. (x0.5)

Fig 3 A typical rewarewa growing in the Otaki Gorge, March 1965.

Fig 4 The tomentose fruits, June. (x0.5)

Family *Protaceae*
Genus *Knightia*

3

4

55

Tutu *Coriaria arborea*

A small, openly-branched tree or shrub with long fern-like leaves, found all over New Zealand from sea level to 1060 m in scrubland, along forest margins, in gullies and on alluvial soils. Tutu is very poisonous, the young shoots as shown in fig 1 being especially so.

Fig 1 A lush young growing shoot.

Fig 2 Flowers of tutu with anthers. (x1)

Fig 3 The dull underside of the leaves. (x1)

Fig 4 Bark from a young tree.

Fig 5 Leaves from above.

Fig 6 A spray of flowers.

Fig 7 The black fruits of tutu.

Family *Coriariaceae*
Genus *Coriaria*

57

Parapara *Pisonia brunoniana*

A small tree to 6 m high with huge leaves up to 40 cm long and sticky fruits that ensnare small birds. Found in coastal areas from Mangonui to East Cape.

4

Fig 1 A parapara tree at Opotiki, December 1974.

Fig 2 The bark of parapara.

Fig 3 The elongated, sticky fruits. (x0.2)

Fig 4 Leaf underside showing shape and venation. (x0.2)

Fig 5 Panicles of flowers, January.

Fig 6 A flower close up, January. (x3)

Family *Nyctaginaceae*
Genus *Pisonia*

5

6

59

Tarata/Lemonwood *Pittosporum eugenioides*

A tree up to 12 m high with a strong lemon-like smell. The largest of the genus *Pittosporum* in New Zealand, it is found all over the country in forests, along forest margins and on stream banks from sea level to 600 m.

2

Fig 1 A mature lemonwood, Taupo, May 1973.

Fig 2 Flowers of lemonwood, October.

Fig 3 A leaf upper side. (x1.5)

Fig 4 The bark of a mature tree.

Fig 5 Last season's ripe fruits on left; this season's green fruits on right; March.

Family *Pittosporaceae*
Genus *Pittosporum*

3

4 5

61

Haekaro *Pittosporum umbellatum* and
  Dall's pittosporum *P. dallii*

1

Both are small, bushy trees 6–8 m high, haekaro occurring down the
east coast from North Cape to Wairoa while Dall's pittosporum is
found only in north-west Nelson.

Fig 1 A fine specimen of haekaro, Opotiki, 1973.

Fig 2 The distinctive, silky, erect hairs on the branchlets and leaf petioles of haekaro. (x4)

Fig 3 Haekaro leaf upper surface.

Fig 4 Many-flowered umbels of haekaro, September. (x0.5)

Fig 5 A leaf of Dall's pittosporum. (x1)

Coromandel pittosporum *Pittosporum huttonianum* and
Northland pittosporums *P. ellipticum* and *P. virgatum*

6

7

A group of upwardly-branching, small trees up to 8 m high found in lowland forests and scrub of Northland and the Coromandel Peninsula. All are characterised by the silky tomentum of the branchlets, leaf petioles and leaf buds.

Fig 1 The leaf upper surface of *P. huttonianum*. (x0.5)

Fig 2 The tangled silky tomentum of *P. huttonianum* branchlets and leaf petioles. (x3)

Fig 3 Leaves of *P. ellipticum* showing golden tomentum beneath.

Fig 4 The thick, golden tomentum clothing the branchlets, leaf petioles and leaf buds of *P. ellipticum* (x 3)

Fig 5 *P. ellipticum* flowers occur as terminal umbels, September. (x2)

Fig 6 *P. virgatum* leaf upper surface. (x1.3)

Fig 7 Spray of *P. virgatum* foliage with seed capsules.

8

Fig 8 The hairy tomentum of *P. virgatum* branchlets, leaf petioles and leaf undersides.

65

Karo *Pittosporum crassifolium*

1

A small tree up to 9 m high with ascending branches. The branchlets, petioles and peduncles are clothed with a dense white or buff tomentum. Found naturally from North Cape to Poverty Bay along coastal streams and forest margins from sea level to 950 m. Now widely spread by cultivation.

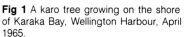

Fig 1 A karo tree growing on the shore of Karaka Bay, Wellington Harbour, April 1965.

Fig 2 The thick leathery leaves. (approx x1)

Fig 3 Leaf underside showing tomentum and rolled edges.

Fig 4 Flowers are in terminal umbels and strongly scented, September. (approx x1)

Fig 5 Karo seed capsules splitting open.

Kohuhu *Pittosporum tenuifolium* and
black mapou *P. tenuifolium* var. *colensoi*

Small trees up to 10 m high with spreading, erect branches. Both are widespread in forests and scrublands throughout New Zealand except that kohuhu does not grow west, and black mapou does not occur east, of the South Island main divide.

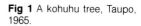

Fig 1 A kohuhu tree, Taupo, 1965.

Fig 2 Kohuhu leaf upper surface. (x1)

Fig 3 Kohuhu leaf lower surface. (x1)

Fig 4 Flowers of kohuhu. (x1)

Fig 5 Bark of kohuhu.

Fig 6 Black mapou leaf spray. (approx x1)

Fig 7 Newly opened black mapou flowers, November. (x3)

Fig 8 Black mapou leaf lower surface. (x0.75)

6

7

8

Karo *Pittosporum ralphii*

1

2

A small tree up to 4 m high, with large leaves 7–12.5 cm long, found along forest margins and streams from Thames south to Dannevirke and Wanganui.

Fig 1 Foliage spray showing tomentum on branchlets and petioles.

Fig 2 Tomentose lower leaf surface with seed capsules, June.

Fig 3 Branchlet, leaf petiole and bud showing dense white tomentum. (x4)

Fig 4 Terminal umbels of flowers, November. (x0.5)

3

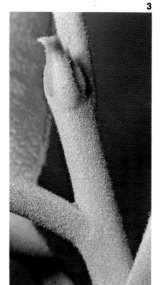

4

Heart-leaved kohuhu   *Pittosporum obcordatum*   and   *P. patulum*

Heart-leaved kohuhu is a narrow, erect, upward-branching tree up to 4 m high occurring in Northland and the East Coast area.

Fig 1 A heart-leaved kohuhu tree growing in Hukutaia Domain, Opotiki, April 1973.

Fig 2 The juvenile foliage of *P. patulum* showing leaf undersides, leaf shapes and leaf arrangement.

Fig 3 Foliage of heart-leaved kohuhu showing leaves and flowers along the branches. (x1)

P. patulum is a small tree up to 5 m high found only in the upper reaches of the Cobb, Wairau and Clarence Rivers. It persists in the juvenile form for many years, and adult trees are very rare.

1

2

3

Pohutukawa *Metrosideros excelsa*

A massive, spreading tree with stout, often horizontally-spreading branches and reaching a height of 20 m with a short thick trunk up to 2 m through. Found along the coasts north of Kawhia and Opotiki.

2

Fig 1 A huge pohutukawa on the Coromandel coast, December 1969.

Fig 2 Pohutukawa flowers, January. (x0.5)

Fig 3 A spray of pohutukawa showing pointed leaf shape, glossy leaf upper surface and tomentum on petiole and leaf lower surface. (approx x1)

Family *Myrtaceae*
Genus *Metrosideros*

3

Rata *Metrosideros robusta*

1   3

2

A rata usually begins life as an epiphyte perched on a host tree. Its aerial roots grow downwards to the ground, finally enclosing the host tree and producing a huge tree up to 25 m high with a trunk up to 2.5 m through. It occurs throughout the North Island and in the South Island south to about Westport.

4

Fig 1 A huge rata at Lake Waikaremoana, January 1966.

Fig 2 The fused, aerial roots of a huge rata at Lake Waikaremoana, showing the hollow left by decay of the host tree.

Fig 3 The bark of rata.

Fig 4 Rata flowers, January. (x2)

Fig 5 The thick, leathery leaf, upper surface. (x1)

Fig 6 The underside of a rata leaf. (x1)

5

6

Southern rata *Metrosideros umbellata*

This tree grows from a seed in the ground to a tree up to 15 m high with a trunk 1 m through. It occurs from sea level to 760 m from Whangarei south to Stewart Island, but is rare in the North Island.

North-west Nelson rata/Shrubby rata *Metrosideros parkinsonii*

A small tree up to 7 m high or a straggling, semi-prostrate shrub, found on Great Barrier Island, in north-west Nelson and the Paparoa Ranges south to Greymouth from sea level to 920 m.

2

3

4

Fig 1 A southern rata tree in full flower on the banks of the Haast River, January 1973.

Fig 2 The pale lower leaf surface with oil glands. (x1)

Fig 3 Leaves and flowers. The flowers are simpler with fewer stamens than those of rata, December. (x0.5)

Fig 4 Typical north-west Nelson rata leaf spray. (x0.5)

Fig 5 The symmetrical flowers of north-west Nelson rata arise in the forks of branches, which have a scaly bark, September. (x0.5)

77

Kanuka *Leptospermum ericoides* and **manuka** *L. scoparium*

1 4

2

Both are small trees or shrubs; kanuka grows to 15 m high with a trunk 60 cm through and manuka grows to 4 m high. Both occur all over New Zealand in forests and scrubland.

78

5

6

Fig 1 A kanuka tree in full flower, Lake Rotoiti, Nelson, January 1972.

Fig 2 A fine kanuka specimen at Ponatahi, September 1968.

Fig 3 A spray of kanuka flowers and leaves.

Fig 4 Kanuka bark. Manuka bark is similar.

Fig 5 Manuka spray.

Fig 6 Underside of manuka leaves showing pungent tips and aromatic glands. (x4)

Fig 7 Manuka flowers, December. (x2.5)

Fig 8 Manuka seed capsules, Hinakura, July. Kanuka seed capsules are similar. (x2)

Family *Myrtaceae*
Genus *Leptospermum*

7

8

Ramarama *Lophomyrtus bullata* and **rohutu** *L. obcordata*

1

Ramarama grows as a small tree up to 6 m high in open forests and along forest margins in coastal forests from sea level to 600 m throughout the North Island, in Nelson, and in Marlborough. Rohutu, forming a smaller tree with thin, upright, clustered branches, is found from Mangonui south throughout New Zealand from sea level to 1,050 m.

2

3

Fig 1 A small ramarama tree, Maungatukutuku Valley, March 1976.

Fig 2 Spray of ramarama foliage with berries; from a tree in shade, June. Trees in the open usually have red-blotched leaves.

Fig 3 Rohutu flowers, December. (Slightly enlarged)

Fig 4 Rohutu leaf undersides. (x4)

Fig 5 The thick, leathery leaves of rohutu, upper sides, and a ripe berry. (x2.5)

Family *Myrtaceae*
Genus *Lophomyrtus*

4

5

Mountain ribbonwoods   *Hoheria lyallii*   and   *H. glabrata*

Two small, spreading, deciduous trees, *H. lyallii* growing to 6 m high and *H. glabrata* to 10 m high. Both are found along forest margins, stream terraces and in shrublands from 600 to 1,050 m altitude in South Island mountains, *H. lyallii* mainly on the eastern side of the main divide and *H. glabrata* on the west side.

Fig 1 A tree of *H. lyallii* growing at Arthurs Pass, January 1967.

Fig 2 Lower surface of leaf of *H. lyallii*. (approx x1)

Fig 3 Upper surface of leaf of *H. glabrata*. (approx x1)

Fig 4 Flowers of *H. glabrata*. Those of *H. lyallii* are similar; both are about 4 cm across.

Family *Malvaceae*
Genus *Hoheria*

82

Narrow-leaved lacebark   *Hoheria angustifolia*

Fig 1 A fine tree in flower at Peel Forest, Canterbury, January 1967.

Fig 2 Juvenile leaves. (approx x1)

Fig 3 A spray of adult leaves showing the pale undersides. (x0.6)

Fig 4 Branchlet showing flowers, buds and leaf upper surfaces. (x0.8)

A slender, spreading tree up to 10 m high, found along forest margins from Taranaki south and throughout the South Island. It passes through a juvenile stage with interlacing branches bearing small leaves.

83

Lacebark/Houhere *Hoheria populnea* and
long-leaved lacebark/houhere *H. sexstylosa*

Family *Malvaceae*
Genus *Hoheria*

Graceful, erect, much-branched trees, the
former up to 11 m high and the latter up to
6 m. *H. populnea* is found naturally only
around Kaitaia and *H. sexstylosa* in forests
and along forest margins from Whangarei
south to Nelson and from Banks Peninsula
to near Gore. Both are now found extensively
in cultivation throughout New Zealand.

84

Fig 1 A typical lacebark, *H. populnea*, Taupo, May 1973.

Fig 2 Spray of *H. populnea* leaves.

Fig 3 Flower of *H. populnea*, Kaitaia, April 1979. There are five carpels. (x2)

Fig 4 Flowers of *H. sexstylosa* var. *ovata*. There are six carpels.

Fig 5 Leaf underside of *H. populnea* (x1)

Fig 6 Leaf spray showing leaf upper surfaces of *H. sexstylosa*. (x0.5)

Fig 7 Leaf lower surfaces of *H. sexstylosa*. (x0.5)

Fig 8 Ripe fruits of *H. populnea*. (x1)

85

Manatu/Ribbonwood *Plagianthus regius*

3

4

2

1

A medium or large tree up to 15 m high with a trunk up to 1 m through. The largest of the New Zealand deciduous trees, manatu is found from Mangonui south throughout the North, South and Stewart Islands on riverbanks and alluvial terraces and along lowland forest margins from sea level to 450 m.

5 6

7

Fig 1 A fine manatu with new spring foliage, Waiorongomai, November 1969.

Fig 2 The bark of manatu.

Fig 3 Leaf upper surface. (approx x1)

Fig 4 Leaf lower surface. (approx x1)

Fig 5 The long, hanging, paniculate cyme of male flowers, October.

Fig 6 Part of a spray of female flowers with fruits forming, November.

Fig 7 Male flowers close up. (x6)

Family *Malvaceae*
Genus *Plagianthus*

Makamaka   *Caldcluvia rosaefolia*

2

A small tree up to 12 m high found in lowland forests between Kaitaia and Whangarei.

Fig 1 The leaf upper surface. (x0.5)

Fig 2 Flowers, August. (x4)

Fig 3 Panicles of seed capsules, August.

Fig 4 The bark of makamaka.

Family *Cunoniaceae*
Genus *Caldcluvia*

1

3

4

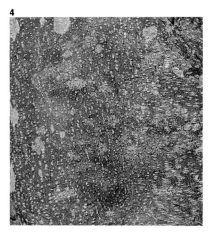

Rohutu   *Neomyrtus pedunculata*

1

A small tree or shrub up to 6 m high
with four-angled branchlets. Found all
over New Zealand from sea level to
1,050 m.

Fig 1 A rohutu tree, Waipunga Gorge, December
1974.

Fig 2 Branchlet with flowers and leaves, January.
(x4)

Fig 3 Branchlet with leaves and berries, April. (x2)

Family *Myrtaceae*
Genus *Neomyrtus*

89

Putaputaweta *Carpodetus serratus*

1

A small tree up to 10 m high with branches spreading outwards in flattened tiers. It is found throughout New Zealand along forest margins and stream banks from sea level to 1,050 m.

2

4

Fig 1 A putaputaweta in flower in the Reikorangi Valley, December 1976.

Fig 2 The underside of a leaf. (x1)

Fig 3 The upper side of a leaf. (x1)

Fig 4 Flowers, December. These occur in panicles. (x6)

Fig 5 Panicles of ripening fruits; these turn black when fully ripe, March.

Family *Escalloniaceae*
Genus *Carpodetus*

3

5

91

Maire tawaki *Syzygium maire*

A canopied tree up to 15 m high, found in swampy and boggy forests throughout the North Island from sea level to 450 m.

Fig 1 A fine maire tawaki growing near Lake Pounui, March 1975.

Fig 2 Flowers and flower buds, Lake Pounui, March. (x1)

Fig 3 A young shoot showing upper and lower leaf surfaces. (x1)

Fig 4 A bunch of berries, March. (x1.75)

Fig 5 The characteristic smooth bark.

Family *Myrtaceae*
Genus *Syzygium*

3

5

Whau   *Entelea arborescens*

Fig 1 A whau growing out from a cliff, Mokau River mouth, December 1973.

A shrub or canopy tree up to 6 m high with a trunk 25 cm through, found in coastal and lowland forests from North Cape south to the Mokau River mouth and the Bay of Plenty. It occurs from sea level to 250 m.

2

4

3

5

6

Fig 2 Leaf upper surface. Leaves are normally 20 cm long but may reach 60 cm. (x0.25)

Fig 3 Leaf lower surface. (x0.25)

Fig 4 Whau flowers, November. (approx x1)

Fig 5 The soft, wrinkled and blistered bark.

Fig 6 Seed capsules opening to reveal their seeds, February. (approx x1)

Family *Tiliaceae*
Genus *Entelea*

Wineberry/Makomako *Aristotelia serrata*

1

A very common, small tree, to 10 m high with a trunk up to 30 cm through, found throughout New Zealand in forests and scrubland, along forest margins and roadsides. In cold areas it is deciduous.

Fig 1 A tree at the side of the Haast Pass road, January 1971.

Fig 2 The leaf lower surface with its pubescent petiole and veins.
Undersides are often reddish-coloured. (x0.75)

Fig 3 Leaf upper surface. (x0.75)

Fig 4 Panicles of ripe berries, March. (approx x1)

Fig 5 A panicle of wineberry flowers, November.

2

3

Family *Elaeocarpaceae*
Genus *Aristotelia*

5

4

Hinau
Elaeocarpus dentatus

A canopy tree, to 18 m high with a trunk up to 1 m through, occurring in lowland forests from sea level to 600 m throughout both the North and South Islands.

Fig 1 Upper surface of leaf. (x1)

Fig 2 Lower surface of leaf. (x1)

Fig 3 Hinau flowers occur as racemes, November. (x2)

Fig 4 Hinau tree in full flower, Reikorangi Valley, December 1977.

Family *Elaeocarpaceae*
Genus *Elaeocarpus*

Pokaka
Elaeocarpus hookerianus

A canopy tree similar in appearance to hinau and reaching up to 12 m high with a trunk 1 m through. It is found in forests and scrubland from sea level to 1,050 m throughout New Zealand.

Fig 1 Branchlet showing leaves and leaf arrangement.

Fig 2 Underside of a pokaka leaf. (x1)

Fig 3 A branch with racemes of flowers, November.

Fig 4 A ripe drupe, March. Hinau drupes are similar. (x3)

Kamahi *Weinmannia racemosa* and **tawhero/towhai** *W. silvicola*

1   2

4

3

5   6

Kamahi forms a spreading tree up to 25 m high with a trunk up to 1.2 m through, found in lowland forests from sea level to 900 m from Auckland south throughout the North, South and Stewart Islands. Tawhero is a canopy-forming tree up to 15 m high with a trunk up to 1 m through, found in forests and along forest margins from Mangonui south to Waikato and the Bay of Plenty.

Fig 1 A fine kamahi tree starting to flower on the Waitaanga Saddle, December 1973.

Fig 2 A spray of kamahi leaves.

Fig 3 Lower surface of kamahi leaf. (x1)

Fig 4 Kamahi flowers and fruits, December. (x0.25)

Fig 5 Spray of tawhero leaves.

Fig 6 Tawhero tree in full flower, Mangamaku Gorge, December 1973.

Fig 7 Tawhero flowers, January. (x0.5)

Family *Cunoniaceae*
Genus *Weinmannia*

7

Tawari   *Ixerba brexioides*

A canopy tree up to 15 m high found in dark shady places in hilly and mountain forest interiors. Occurs in the North Island from about Cape Brett to the Urewera, up to 900 m altitude.

3

Family *Escalloniaceae*
Genus *Ixerba*

4

Fig 1 A tawari tree exposed on the Mamaku Plateau by forest clearing, October 1965.

Fig 2 A tawari leaf, upper side. (x1)

Fig 3 A panicle of flowers nestles among leaves at the apex of a branchlet, December. (x2)

Fig 4 Leaf undersides showing teeth, each tipped by a gland. (x0.5)

Fig 5 Ripe seed capsules, six months after pollination, alongside the new season's flower buds, May.

5

103

Westland quintinia *Quintinia acutifolia* and
tawherowhero *Q. serrata*

2

Westland quintinia is a bushy
forest tree up to 12 m high,
found from Coromandel, the
Barrier islands and the National
Park area to Taranaki in the
North Island and from north-
west Nelson to Westland in the
South Island. Tawherowhero is
an open-branching forest tree up
to 9 m high found only from
Mangonui to Taranaki and
Poverty Bay.

1

3

Fig 1 A tree of Westland quintinia from Gillespie's Bush, Fox Glacier, 1973.

Fig 2 Upper surface of a Westland quintinia leaf. (x0.5)

Fig 3 Racemes of Westland quintinia flowers arise in the axils of the leaves towards the tips of the branchlets, November.

Fig 4 A spray of tawherowhero leaves showing alternate arrangement.

Fig 5 Undersurface of a tawherowhero leaf. (approx x1)

Fig 6 A tawherowhero flower panicle, October. (x3)

Fig 7 Tawherowhero seed capsules, December. (x3)

Family *Escalloniaceae*
Genus *Quintinia*

Kowhai *Sophora tetraptera*

1

The North Island kowhai *S. tetraptera* is found growing wild along streams and forest margins from East Cape to the Ruahine Range between sea level and 450 m. It is a small, spreading tree up to 12 m high which is now cultivated and grown throughout New Zealand.

2

3

4

Fig 1 Kowhai in flower, Lake Taupo, October 1968.

Fig 2 Leaves of *S. tetraptera* each have 10–20 pairs of leaflets.

Fig 3 Flowers of *S. tetraptera* showing the long keel, shorter wings and even shorter standard, September. (approx x1)

Fig 4 Seed pods of *S. tetraptera*. (approx x1)

Fig 5 The bark of *S. tetraptera*.

Family *Papilionaceae*
Genus *Sophora*

5

107

Kowhai *Sophora microphylla* and **prostrate kowhai** *S. prostrata*

1

S. microphylla is a smaller, more feathery-looking tree than *S. tetraptera*, reaching 10 m high and found throughout the country along river banks and forest margins and in open places. Like *S. tetraptera* it is now widely distributed in cultivation.

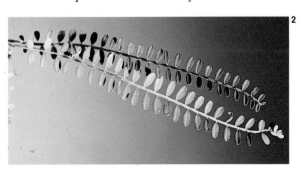

2

3

4

Fig 1 A tree of *S. microphylla* growing on the Kaikoura Coast, December 1964.

Fig 2 Leaves of *S. microphylla* each have 20–40 pairs of leaflets.

Fig 3 Portion of a leaf of *S. microphylla* var. *fulvida* with its hairy leaflets and rachis covered with a dense golden-brown tomentum. (x4)

Fig 4 Flowers of *S. microphylla* with the wings and standard of equal length and the keel only slightly longer than the standard, October. (x1)

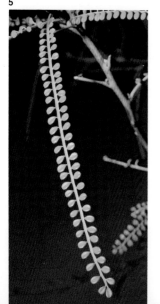

5

6

Fig 5 A leaf of *S. microphylla* var. *longicarinata*, which grows to a length of 20 cm.

Fig 6 Flowers and leaves of the prostrate kowhai, *S. prostrata*, September. The keel of the flower is noticeably longer than either the wings or the standard. The leaves each have 6–8 pairs of leaflets. *S. prostrata* grows to 2 m high and is found in open rocky or grassy places in the South Island from north-west Nelson to Canterbury.

109

Tree broom/Weeping broom *Chordospartium stevensonii*

A tree up to 9 m high with an umbrella-like canopy of drooping branchlets. Found growing on silty flats in river valleys of Marlborough.

2

4

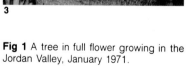

3

Fig 1 A tree in full flower growing in the Jordan Valley, January 1971.

Fig 2 The grooved bark of a seedling tree about seven years old.

Fig 3 The bark of a mature tree showing typical transverse rings and traces of juvenile grooves.

Fig 4 A typical curved flower raceme arising from a node on a branchlet, December. (approx x1)

Family *Papilionaceae*
Genus *Chordospartium*

111

Pink tree broom *Notospartium glabrescens*

Found only in Marlborough, growing in rocky situations from sea level to 1,200 m, pink broom when in flower is one of New Zealand's most spectacular plants.

Fig 1 A beautiful tree of pink broom in flower, Woodside Gorge, December 1969.

Fig 2 A raceme of flowers, December. (x2)

Fig 3 The bark of growing stems is at first "ropey" but later becomes smoother.

Family *Papilionaceae*
Genus *Notospartium*

Native tree brooms *Carmichaelia* species

1 **2**

Five species of native tree brooms are found throughout New Zealand. All have rounded, compressed, or flattened, green branchlets which perform the functions of leaves. True leaves occur more commonly on seedlings or on plants growing in shade.

Fig 1 Scented broom, *C. odorata* is found along streams and forest margins from Tolaga Bay south from sea level to 750 m. The strongly emarginate leaves are 5–7 foliate and the drooping stems are flattened and grooved.

Fig 2 Giant-flowered broom *C. williamsii* grows to 4 m high and is found in coastal areas of Bay of Plenty and East Cape. Now grown extensively in gardens.

Fig 3 South Island broom *C. arborea* forms a tree up to 5 m high with ascending branches and compressed, straight branchlets. Found mainly in the west of the South Island along streams, forest margins and on alluvial ground.

Fig 4 North Island broom *C. aligera* grows to 10 m high and is found from Northland south to Taranaki, mainly along forest margins. The photo shows the seed pods. (x1)

Fig 5 Leafy broom *C. angustata* reaches 2 m high and is found along streams and forest margins in southern Marlborough and from Karamea south to Hokitika. This broom always has a few leaves which, along with the branchlets, are hairy.

Family *Papilionaceae*
Genus *Carmichaelia*

3 **4** **5**

New Zealand beeches
Nothofagus species

These are tall forest trees that grow as extensive, pure or mixed stands, from sea level to 1,200 m in the north, descending to sea level in the far south of the South Island. Beeches do not grow on Mt Egmont or Stewart Island.

Silver beech/Tawhai *Nothofagus menziesii* and hard beech/tawhairaunui *N. truncata*

In the forest, silver beech forms a tall tree with tiered branches reaching 30 m high and a trunk 2 m across, but in the open it is broad, spreading and dome-shaped. Found from Thames south, from sea level to 900 m.

Hard beech is a tree up to 30 m high, with a trunk up to 2 m through which is often strongly buttressed. It is found from Mangonui south to Greymouth and the Wairau River, from sea level to 900 m.

Fig 1 A typical silver beech photographed in Kaimanawa Forest Park, December 1973.

Fig 2 Underside of a silver beech leaf, showing vein pattern, thick edges, and two domatia. (x3)

Fig 3 Gland-dotted upper sides of two silver beech leaves. (x3)

Fig 4 A female flower of silver beech, January. (x2)

Fig 5 Seed cupules of silver beech, January. (x2)

Fig 6 Male flowers and truncated leaves of hard beech.

Fig 7 The lower surface of hard beech leaves. (approx x1)

Family *Fagaceae*
Genus *Nothofagus*

115

Red beech/Tawhairaunui *Nothofagus fusca*

Red beech occurs from Te Aroha south to Fiordland, from sea level to 1,050 m. It reaches 30 m high with a trunk 2–3 m through. Juvenile trees are characterised by their deep red foliage during the winter.

2

3

Fig 1 A fine specimen of red beech from the Hutt Valley, December 1973.

Fig 2 The underside of a red beech leaf showing venation and three domatia. (x1.4)

Fig 3 The typical, alternate leaves of red beech. (approx x1)

Fig 4 Beech trees flower at irregular intervals, but when they do they make a spectacular sight with flowers in great profusion. These are the male flowers of a black beech from the Rimutaka Hill, October 1965.

4

Black beech/Tawhairauriki *Nothofagus solandri*

This beech is found from southern Waikato and East Cape south in both the North and South Islands, from sea level to 750 m. It reaches 25 m high with a trunk up to 1 m through.

Fig 1 A leaf spray of black beech. (x1.5)

Fig 2 The underside of a black beech leaf showing whitish hairs along veins. (x5)

Mountain beech/Tawhairauriki *Nothofagus solandri*
var. *cliffortioides*

A smaller tree reaching to 15 m high, found growing in mountain and subalpine forest from sea level to 1,200 m.

Fig 3 The leaf upper surface of mountain beech. (x3)

Fig 4 Mountain beech leaves showing the rolled-down margins and densely pubescent lower surfaces.(x3)

118

Ongaonga/tree nettle *Urtica ferox*

1 2

A shrub or small tree up to 3 m high with a trunk 12 cm across, found throughout the North Island and along the west coast of the South Island.

Fig 1 A branchlet showing stinging hairs. (x3.5)

Fig 2 A shrubby form of ongaonga showing the interlacing branches, Gladstone, 1972.

Fig 3 The upper surface of a leaf, with male flowers arising in the leaf axil. (x0.75)

Fig 4 Female flower spikes. (x0.25)

3 4

Family *Urticaceae*
Genus *Urtica*

119

Towai/Large-leaved milk tree *Paratrophis banksii* and turepo/small-leaved milk tree *P. microphylla*

3

4

Family *Moraceae*
Genus *Paratrophis*

2   1

120

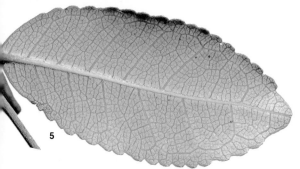

5

8

6

Towai is a canopy tree up to 12 m high with a short trunk while turepo is a slender tree, also about 12 m high. Both have a trunk about 60 cm through and are found in lowland forests up to 450 m altitude, towai south from Mangonui to the Marlborough Sounds and turepo throughout both the North and South Islands.

Fig 1 A turepo tree, Waiorongomai, 1968.

Fig 2 Juvenile leaf of turepo. (x8)

Fig 3 A typical turepo leaf, upper side. (x2)

Fig 4 The underside of a turepo leaf. (x2)

Fig 5 The underside of a towai leaf. (x1.3)

Fig 6 A towai spray showing leaf upper sides and male flower spikes.

Fig 7 Male flower spikes of towai arise laterally and sometimes terminally. (x1.3)

Fig 8 The ripe drupes of towai. (x0.75)

Fig 9 Flower spike of female turepo. (x5)

7

9

Karaka *Corynocarpus laevigatus*

1

2

A handsome leafy canopy tree growing to 15 m high with a smooth trunk up to 60 cm across. Karaka grows in coastal regions, often in groves, throughout New Zeala

122

3

4

5

Fig 1 A karaka growing at Ngunguru, 1970.

Fig 2 The lower surface of a karaka leaf. (x0.5)

Fig 3 Upper surface of a karaka leaf. (x1)

Fig 4 Karaka drupes, February. (approx x1)

Fig 5 A panicle of karaka flowers, October. (approx x1)

Family *Corynocarpaceae*
Genus *Corynocarpus*

123

Kaikomako *Pennantia corymbosa*

A slender tree up to 12 m high which passes through a straggling, twiggy, interlacing, juvenile stage that lasts for many years. Found from sea level to 600 m in forests throughout New Zealand.

Fig 1 A kaikomako in flower, Lake Pounui, 1972.

Fig 2 Panicles of male flowers and buds, December.

Fig 3 A juvenile kaikomako, Opepe Bush, 1978.

Fig 4 Juvenile leaves. (approx x1)

Fig 5 Kaikomako drupes are shining black when fully ripe, March.

Family *Icacinaceae*
Genus *Pennantia*

124

3

4

5

Maire *Mida salicifolia*

A slender tree up to 6 m high with a trunk up to 20 cm through, found rather locally in lowland and lower montane forest from sea level to 450 m throughout New Zealand but more common in the north.

126

5

6

Fig 1 Two maire trees growing in the Rewa Reserve, 1973.

Fig 2 The inflorescences arise from the leaf axils, October.

Fig 3 Ripening fruits, October. (approx x1)

Fig 4 The bark is very rough.

Fig 5 Functionally male flowers, October. (x5)

Fig 6 Leaves from northern trees tend to be broader than those from southern trees.

Fig 7 A spray of narrow leaves.

Fig 8 Leaves may be opposite, or alternate as here.

Family *Santalaceae*
Genus *Mida*

7

8

Kumarahou/Golden tainui *Pomaderris kumeraho* and *P. hamiltonii*

Fig 1 P. kumeraho in full flower.

Fig 2 Upper surface of the soft *P. kumeraho* leaf. (x1)

Fig 3 A spray of *P. hamiltonii* showing leaf undersides.

Fig 4 Leaf spray of *P. hamiltonii* showing upper surfaces and some developing flower buds of the much more open flower corymbs of this species.

Both species grow as small slender trees or shrubs 3–4 m high in scrubland from North Cape south to the Bay of Plenty.

Family *Rhamnaceae*
Genus *Pomaderris*

128

Tainui   *Pomaderris apetala*

2

3

4

1

An erect, branching, small tree or shrub up to 5 m high, found naturally in coastal localities from Kawhia south to the Mokau River. Often grown in parks and gardens.

Fig 1 A tainui tree growing at Otari, 1970.

Fig 2 Tomentose branchlet and leaves showing upper surfaces.

Fig 3 The lower surface of a leaf. (x1)

Fig 4 The spectacular flower head is about 10 cm long, November.

Poataniwha   *Melicope simplex*

2

1

3

A small tree or shrub up to 8 m high with divaricating branches, found along coastal or lowland forest margins throughout the North and South Islands.

Fig 1 A small tree at Opotiki, 1974.

Fig 2 Leaf underside dotted with aromatic glands. (x2)

Fig 3 Opening seed capsules, April.

Fig 4 Female flowers, November. (x8)

Family *Rutaceae*   Genus *Melicope*

Wharangi   *Melicope ternata*

A stiffly branched, small tree up to 7 m high found from sea level to 300 m along forest margins, in scrub and in rocky places, from North Cape south to Nelson.

Fig 1 A spray showing leaves and flower cymes and flowers and buds, September.

Fig 2 Seed capsules of a poataniwha/wharangi hybrid. Such hybridisation is fairly common.

Fig 3 Branchlet showing the trifoliate leaves. (x1)

Fig 4 A wharangi tree leaning towards the light, Waikanae, 1979.

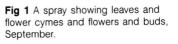

Kohekohe *Dysoxylum spectabile*

1

A spreading canopy tree up to 15 m high with a trunk up to 1 m through, found in damp situations in coastal forests from North Cape south to Nelson. The long panicles of flowers which sprout directly from the trunk and branches make it a most spectacular tree.

2

Family *Meliaceae*
Genus *Dysoxylum*

3

Fig 1 A large kohekohe tree growing at Waikanae, 1973.

Fig 2 Clusters of panicles of flowers sprout from the trunk of a kohekohe, May.

Fig 3 The upper side of some of the leaflets which make up the large, pinnately-compound kohekohe leaf. (x0.5)

Fig 4 An individual flower showing the thick, waxy petals and greenish sepals. (x2)

Fig 5 A short panicle of mature seed capsules, May. (x1)

5

4

Titoki *Alectryon excelsus*

2

1

3

4

5

6

With its short, stout trunk, this spreading tree, reaching a height of 10 m, is found in lowland forests from sea level to 600 m from North Cape to Banks Peninsula and Bruce Bay.

Fig 1 A titoki tree growing at Hinakura, 1964.

Fig 2 Upper side of a typical titoki leaf. (x0.12)

Fig 3 A panicle of seed capsules, December (x1)

Fig 4 A spray showing young leaves with flower panicles arising from the leaf axils.

Fig 5 The apex of a flower panicle, November. (x0.5)

Fig 6 A male flower shedding pollen, November. (x9.5)

Family *Sapindaceae*
Genus *Alectryon*

135

Akeake *Dodonaea viscosa*

A small, erect tree or shrub up to 7 m high with spreading, gently ascending branches and sticky branchlets. Found from sea level to 550 m in coastal and lowland scrub and forests from North Cape south to Banks Peninsula and about Greymouth.

Fig 1 A typical akeake growing in the East Takaka Valley, 1971.

Fig 2 A leaf upper surface. (approx x1)

Fig 3 A leaf lower surface. (approx x1)

Fig 4 The flaking, papery bark.

Family *Sapindaceae*
Genus *Dodonaea*

136

5

7

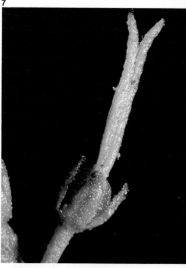

8

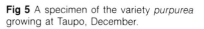

Fig 5 A specimen of the variety *purpurea* growing at Taupo, December.

Fig 6 Seed capsules of var. *purpurea*.

Fig 7 A typical flower panicle of akeake.

Fig 8 A single female flower, October (x9).

Fig 9 Seed capsules of akeake.

9

Pate   *Schefflera digitata*

Throughout New Zealand from sea level to 1,200 m, pate is found in damp parts of forests and along stream banks or shady roadsides as a small, spreading tree up to 8 m high.

Fig 1 A branch photographed from below to show the leaf undersides, prominent leaflet midveins and the long, stout petioles of the compound leaves.

Fig 2 The central leaflet of the compound leaf. (approx x1)

Fig 3 A pate tree growing on the Rahu Saddle, 1973.

Fig 4 An inflorescence of pate, February.

Fig 5 Underside of the leaf of the juvenile form of pate. (x0.3)

Family *Araliaceae*
Genus *Schefflera*

139

Five-finger/Puahou *Pseudopanax arboreus*

3

1

2

4

One of the commonest of our native trees, five-finger is found from sea level to 760 m in forests and open scrub from North Cape to Southland. It reaches 8 m in height and is characterised by its leaf of 5–7 leaflets each with a petiolule, the whole being on a petiole up to 20 cm long.

Family *Araliaceae*
Genus *Pseudopanax*

140

5

Fig 1 A very old five-finger growing in the Waipahihi Reserve, Taupo, 1973.

Fig 2 A typical five-finger leaf. (x0.3)

Fig 3 A single male flower, August. (x5)

Fig 4 Female flowers, August. (x5)

Fig 5 The normal rounded form of the young tree, Lake Taupo, 1965.

Fig 6 Male flowers and buds smothering the foliage in typical fashion, Taupo, August.

6

Fig 1 A small tree showing the reddish-coloured midveins and petioles of the leaves.

A small tree up to 5 m high, found from Coromandel south to Taranaki along forest margins and in forests or scrub. It is similar in appearance to five-finger but easily distinguished by its red-coloured leaf petioles and leaf midveins.

Orihou *Pseudopanax colensoi*

A small canopy tree with stout, spreading branches, found from sea level to 1,200 m in forests, scrub and subalpine scrub throughout New Zealand. Distingushed from five-finger by the leaflets, which have a short petiolule or none at all.

Fig 1 A small tree of orihou growing above the Kauaeranga Valley, 1970.

Fig 2 Upper surface of the thick, leathery subsessile leaflets. (approx x1)

Fig 3 A complete leaf with sessile leaflets. (x0.5)

143

Lancewood/Horoeka   *Pseudopanax crassifolius*

Fig 1 Juvenile forms at left and right foreground, with an adult tree in centre and a juvenile changing to adult behind it, Pelorus Bridge, 1972.

The mature lancewood is a round-headed tree up to 15 m high with a straight trunk up to 50 cm through. It is found in forest and scrubland throughout New Zealand from sea level to 760 m. The thick, leathery, upright leaves reach to 20 cm in length, contrasting with the juvenile leaves that reach to 1 m in length and are reflexed downwards.

Fig 2 A mature lancewood, Hinakura, 1970.

Fig 3 Upper surface of adult leaves. (x0.6)

Fig 4 Lancewood fruits, March.

3 4

145

Toothed lancewood *Pseudopanax ferox*

Fig 1 A mature and a semi-mature toothed lancewood at Otari, 1973.

Fig 2 Two juvenile toothed lancewoods, Otari, 1973.

A bushy-topped tree reaching to 6 m with a tall, slender trunk branching at the top. Toothed lancewood trees are found from sea level to 900 m in scattered groups, from Mangonui south to Otago.

Fig 3 Juvenile leaves.

Fig 4 The trunk of toothed lancewood has characteristic rounded, swollen ridges.

Pseudopanax discolor and *P. gilliesii*

Fig 1 A leaf of *P. discolor*, upper surface. (x1)

Fig 2 Undersurface of a trifoliolate leaf of *P. discolor*. (x0.5)

Both grow as shrubs or small trees 5–6 m high in lowland or coastal forests and scrub, *P. discolor* occurring from Mangonui to Thames and *P. gilliesii* from North Cape to Whangaroa. Both have thick leaves on long petioles, the former having 3–5 and the latter one or three leaflets.

Fig 3 A spray of *P. gilliesii* showing both unifoliolate and trifoliolate leaves.

Houpara *Pseudopanax lessonii*

1 2

A shrub or small tree 5–6 m high found in coastal forest and scrub from North Cape to Poverty Bay.

Fig 1 A spray of houpara foliage showing the thick, leathery leaves on long petioles.

Fig 2 Upper surface of a leaf. (x0.5)

Fig 3 A houpara tree showing the leaves crowded towards the tips of the branches, Kauaeranga Valley, 1970.

Haumakaroa   *Pseudopanax simplex*

A much-branched shrub or small tree up to 8 m high, found from sea level to 1,200 m in forest from about Thames south to Stewart Island. Adult trees have unifoliolate leaves but juveniles are three to five-foliolate.

Fig 1 Lower surface of a leaf. (approx x1)

Fig 2 Upper surface of an adult leaf. (approx x1)

Fig 3 A spray of haumakaroa with juvenile trifoliolate leaves and adult unifoliolate leaves.

149

Raukawa *Pseudopanax edgerleyi*

Fig 1 Upper surface of a typical raukawa leaf. (approx x1)

Fig 2 A bifoliolate leaf, lower surface. (approx x1)

A forest tree up to 10 m high with a trunk up to 40 cm through, found from Mangonui south to Stewart Island between sea level and 600 m. Adult leaves are unifoliolate or bifoliolate and aromatic. Juvenile plants have three to five-foliolate leaves with the leaflets deeply lobed. All leaves have very long petioles, up to 15 cm.

3

Fig 3 A spray of foliage with uni- and tri-foliolate leaves.

Fig 4 Flower umbels occur on slender, branched stalks 5 cm long.

Fig 5 A trifoliolate leaf from a juvenile plant. (approx x1)

4

5

151

Papauma/Broadleaf *Griselinia littoralis* and **puka** *G. lucida*

1

Broadleaf grows as a spreading tree up to 15 m high and is found from sea level to 900 m in forest from Mangonui south throughout New Zealand. Puka grows first as an epiphyte perched high on rimu, kahikatea, hinau, kohekohe, puriri or cabbage trees. Puka occurs in lowland forests throughout both the North and South Islands.

2

3

Fig 1 A broadleaf tree, Canaan, 1965.

Fig 2 Flowers of broadleaf arise as panicles from the leaf axils towards the branchlet tips, April.

Fig 3 The furrowed, blistery bark of broadleaf.

Fig 4 Leaves of broadleaf, upper side. (approx x1)

Fig 5 The asymmetric leaf bases typical of puka. (x0.5)

Fig 6 Ripening fruits of broadleaf, March.

Family *Cornaceae*
Genus *Griselinia*

Mingimingi *Leucopogon fasciculatus*

An openly branched, small tree or shrub, 5–6 m high, found from sea level to 1,150 m in forests, scrub and rocky places from North Cape south to Canterbury.

Fig 1 A rather bent tree growing near Taupo, 1973.

Fig 2 Mingimingi leaves, upper and lower surfaces, showing pubescent branchlets, finely serrated hairy margins and pungent tips. (x2)

Fig 3 A drooping raceme of flowers, October. (x2)

Fig 4 Ripening fruits, April. (x3.5)

Family *Epacridaceae*   Genus *Leucopogon*

Matagouri/Wild Irishman   *Discaria toumatou*

A branching shrub or small tree up to 6 m high, found in open tussock, dune country and rocky places from sea level to 900 m. Abundant along the east of the South Island but occurs only sparsely along the west of both the North and South Islands.

Fig 1 A tree growing near Lake Pukaki, 1964.

Fig 2 The rough, chunky bark.

Fig 3 Matagouri in full flower and showing the stiff, hard thorns that arise along the branchlets.

Fig 4 A branchlet showing fascicles of flowers and leaves, October.

Family *Rhamnaceae*   Genus *Discaria*

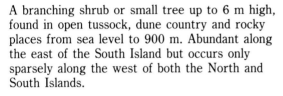

Grass trees genus *Dracophyllum*

Family *Epacridaceae*
Genus *Dracophyllum*

The genus Dracophyllum in New Zealand contains twelve species
that grow as small trees. Leaves of some species pass gradually from
the sheath into the leaf blade (Fig 1, *D. traversii*) while others
develop a distinct shoulder as in Fig 2 (*D. lessonianum*). This
shoulder structure is useful in identification of the species.

1 2

Grass tree *Dracophyllum pyramidale*

A slender, upright tree up to 10 m high, with ascending branches
bearing candelabra-like clusters of thick, leathery leaves towards
their tips. Found in forest and scrubland from Great Barrier Island
south to the Kaimai Ranges and the Urewera.

Fig 3 The characteristic striped bark of
D. pyramidale.

Fig 4 A branchlet tip showing bases of
leaves and their clasping sheath 5 cm long.
Leaves are 50–60 cm long and 2.5–3 cm wide.

Fig 5 A typical *D. pyramidale* tree growing in the forest on Mt Ngamoto, 1974.

Neinei/Spiderwood *Dracophyllum latifolium*

An open, branched, small tree, to 7 m high, with candelabra-like, dense leaf clusters, found from sea level to 1,100 m in forests from Mangonui south to North Taranaki and the Mahia Peninsula.

Fig 1 A typical neinei, Mt Kaitarakihi, 1974.

Fig 2 The finely serrated leaf margin; leaves are 25–60 cm long and 2.5–3.5 cm wide with tapering pointed tips.

Fig 3 The seed panicle of neinei, March. (x6)

Mountain neinei   *Dracophyllum traversii*

1 **2** **3**

A stoutly branching tree reaching to 13 m high with a trunk to 60 cm through. Found between 760 and 1,400 m in forest and scrub from Nelson to about Arthur's Pass.

Fig 1 A fine specimen on Mt Arthur, Nelson, 1972.

Fig 3 The typical peeling bark of *D. traversii*.

Fig 2 A seed head, January.

Dracophyllum mathewsii, D. townsonii and *D. fiordense*

Fig 1 *D. mathewsii* is rather similar to grass tree, but is found only in forests of Northland between Kaitaia and Hokianga. The leaves are 20–30 cm long and 1–2.5 cm wide with smooth margins and acute tips.

Fig 2 Part of the crenate margin of the leaf of *D. townsonii*. (x6) This species, rather like neinei in general appearance, grows to 6 m high with leaves 15–30 cm long by 8–15 mm wide. It is found in lowland forests and scrub from south-west Nelson to north Westland.

Fig 3 A tree of *D. fiordense* which grows to 3 m high with only a single trunk topped by a dense leaf cluster. Leaves are 60–70 cm long by 4–5 cm wide. It is found only in scrub from sea level to 1,050 m through western Otago and Fiordland.

Dracophyllum viride, D. sinclairii and D. lessonianum

1 2   **3**

D. viride forms a slender, upright, branching tree up to 5 m high with leaves 5–7 cm long by 5–6.5 mm wide and a shoulder on the sheath.

Fig 1 The juvenile form, with an angled shoulder on its leaf base (x4.5). The species is found near Kaitaia.

Fig 2 The adult form, with a more round-shaped shoulder and serrulate margins. (x2.5)

Fig 3 The leaf shoulder of *D. sinclairii.* (x2)

D. sinclairii is a slender, much-branched, leafy tree to 6 m high, found in scrub or forest from Kaitaia south to Kawhia and Rotorua.

4

D. lessonianum is a small tree up to 10 m high, with ascending branches and needle-like leaves 6–10 cm long and 1–1.5 mm wide, found in scrub from North Cape south to Kawhia.

Fig 4 The leaf shoulder and serrulated leaf margin of *D. lessonianum.* (x6)

5

Fig 5 A tree of *D. lessonianum* amongst manuka scrub, Kaitaia, 1979.

161

Inanga   *Dracophyllum longifolium*

1

2

3

This is the most widespread dracophyllum, found in coastal, lowland and subalpine scrub and forest from East Cape south throughout New Zealand. It grows to 12 m high with slender, erect or spreading branches and branchlets. The leaves are 10–25 cm long by 3–5 mm wide tapering to a long acuminate tip with the margin smooth or minutely serrulate.

Fig 1 Flower racemes of inanga are typical of most dracophyllums, December. (x0.3)

Fig 2 The leaf shoulder of inanga. (x5)

Fig 3 A leaf tuft of inanga.

162

Dracophyllum filifolium

1 2

A small tree to 2 m high with slender, erect branches and thin, flexible branchlets. Found in montane and subalpine rocky places, fellfields and scrub of the North Island from the Huirau Range southwards. The needle-like leaves are 10–16 cm long by 0.5–1 mm wide, with a three-faced, finely serrated apex.

3

Fig 1 A spray showing leaves and thin flexible branchlets.

Fig 2 The shoulder of the leaf sheath. (x5)

Fig 3 The typically serrulate leaf margins. (x7.5)

163

Tawapou *Planchonella costata*

A small, closely-branched tree up to 15 m high with a trunk up to 1 m through. It grows sporadically on islands and headlands from North Cape south to Tolaga Bay and Manukau Harbour. When cut or broken the branchlets bleed a milky latex.

Fig 1 A specimen of tawapou growing at Martins Bay, near Warkworth, 1971.

Fig 2 The shining mature leaves and pubescent young foliage of tawapou.

3

Fig 3 A spray showing alternate leaf arrangement, pubescent branchlet and leaf petioles and axillary flowers, January.

Fig 4 The distinctive berries at various stages of ripening; each berry contains up to four hard, smooth, curved seeds.

Fig 5 A pubescent branchlet with two petioles and two flower buds in the leaf axils. (x4)

Family *Sapotaceae*
Genus *Planchonella*

4

5

165

Mapou/Mapau/Red matipo   *Myrsine australis*

A shrub or small tree up to 6 m high, with reddish-coloured bark on the young branches and branchlets, while the bark of the trunk of mature trees is grey. Mapou is found from sea level to 900 m throughout New Zealand along forest margins, in scrublands and sometimes inside forests.

Fig 1 An unusual forked tree of mapou growing at Hinakura, 1964.

Fig 2 A close view of male flowers, December. (x12)

Fig 3 A cluster of female flowers showing the large, fringed stigmas, January. (x6)

Fig 4 A branchlet of mapou showing alternate leaf arrangement, red branchlet and petioles and hairy leaf midvein.

Fig 5 Mature drupes cluster around a branchlet, April. (approx x1)

Family *Myrsinaceae*   Genus *Myrsine*

Toro *Myrsine salicina*

2

3

A rather fresh-looking, attractive, open-branched tree up to 8 m high with thick, leathery leaves and thick, furrowed bark. Toro grows from sea level to 850 m in forests from North Cape south to about Greymouth, being more common in the North Island.

Fig 1 A specimen of toro in flower, Tararua Forest Park,1965.

Fig 2 The young shoot and reddish-tinged branchlet characteristic of toro.

Fig 3 A spray of toro foliage.

Fig 4 Flowers clustered round a branchlet, November. As the bark ages it turns black or dark red-brown. (x0.6)

Fig 5 Toro drupes; the red ones are ripe, December. (x0.5)

4

5

169

Weeping matipo *Myrsine divaricata*

A small tree up to 4 m high or a shrub with rigid, spreading branches and stiff, drooping branchlets that are hairy when young. Found from sea level to 1,200 m on forest margins, in scrublands or along river and stream banks throughout New Zealand.

Fig 1 The typical drooping twiggy form of the tree, Lewis Pass, 1973.

Fig 2 The thick, gland-dotted leaf, upper surface. (x2)

Fig 3 Branchlet with ripe drupes and leaf undersides. (x0.5)

Fig 4 Close view of a male flower, September. (x12)

Hangehange   *Geniostoma rupestre*

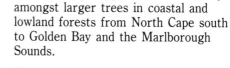

A bushy, much-branching shrub or small tree up to 4 m high, found abundantly amongst larger trees in coastal and lowland forests from North Cape south to Golden Bay and the Marlborough Sounds.

Fig 1 A small tree growing in forest.

Fig 2 A spray of hangehange foliage showing opposite leaves each up to 7 cm long.

Fig 3 Spray showing leaf undersides and the smooth shining nature of the branchlets and leaves.

Fig 4 Hangehange flowers, October. (x2)

Fig 5 Seed capsules up to 7 mm long are borne in profusion, February.

Family *Loganiaceae*
Genus *Geniostoma*

171

Black maire/maire *Nestegis cunninghamii*

1

A tall canopy tree up to 20 m high with a trunk up to 1.5 m through, covered by rough, corky bark. Found from sea level to 760 m throughout the forests of the North Island and Marlborough and Nelson.

Fig 1 A large black maire tree growing on Mt Ruapehu, 1972.

Fig 2 A spray of black maire leaves showing dark upper and pale lower surfaces. Leaves are leathery and up to 15 cm long.

Fig 3 The rough, corky bark.

Fig 4 A male flower, September. (x4)

Fig 5 A female flower showing its large, two-lobed stigma, September. (x4)

Fig 6 Ripe drupes, with next season's drupes forming in racemes above, October. (x0.5)

Family *Oleaceae*
Genus *Nestegis*

White maire *Nestegis lanceolata* and
oro-oro/narrow-leaved maire *N. montana*

White maire is a tall canopy tree up to 15 m high with a trunk 1 m through, found in lowland forests throughout the North Island and in Nelson from sea level to 600 m. Oro-oro forms a much-branched, round-headed tree up to 15 m high with a short trunk 60 cm through. Found from sea level to 600 m from Mangonui south to Nelson and Marlborough.

6

7

Fig 1 A white maire (tall) and an oro-oro tree (shorter, on right) growing in the Waipunga Gorge, 1973.

Fig 2 A spray of white maire showing leaves (up to 12 cm long), female flower racemes and drupes from the previous season.

Fig 3 Ripening drupes of white maire, December. (x2)

Fig 4 A spray of white maire foliage.

Fig 5 A spray of oro-oro foliage; the leaves are up to 9 cm long.

Fig 6 The rough, furrowed bark of white maire.

Fig 7 Racemes of oro-oro male flowers, October. (x5)

Coastal maire *Nestegis apetala*

1

A small tree up to 6 m high, sometimes a shrub, with spreading, often tortuous branches and furrowed bark. It is found growing on rocky headlands around Whangarei and the Bay of Islands.

Fig 1 A small tree of coastal maire growing at Oke Bay, 1978.

Fig 2 The leaf underside. (x1)

Fig 3 Racemes of female flowers arise from leaf axils and directly from the branchlets. Neither male nor female flowers have petals. (x1)

Fig 4 Spray showing leaf upper sides. (x1)

Fig 5 The beautiful drupes of coastal maire, December. (x1.5)

Fig 6 A raceme of male flowers with anthers distended with pollen, January. (x1.75)

177

The genus *Coprosma*

Of the forty-five species of *Coprosma* found in the New Zealand region fifteen grow as small trees 3–6 m high on the mainland. Some are upright and slender (p 182 fig 4), others bushy. (p 186 fig 1) They have characteristic male and female flowers on separate trees (p 179 figs 4 and 5); they all bear drupes, often in great profusion (p 179 fig 3), that vary in colour from white, blue or yellow to orange-red and red. Their opposite stipulate leaves mostly bear domatia in the angles of the veins. (p 178 fig 1) The form of the stipule (P181 fig 6) is characteristic for each species and is a useful diagnostic feature.

Karamu *Coprosma lucida*

Found throughout New Zealand from sea level to 1,060 m in forest, along forest margins and in scrub.

Fig 1 Leaf underside showing domatia. (approx x1)

Fig 2 A foliage spray showing male flower clusters and buds.

Fig 3 Karamu drupes, April. (approx x1)

Fig 4 Karamu male flowers. (x1)

Fig 5 Karamu female flowers. (x1)

Fig 6 The stipule of karamu; the main stem is in the centre with leaf petioles and stems on either side. (x3)

Family *Rubiaceae*
Genus *Coprosma*

3

4 5

6

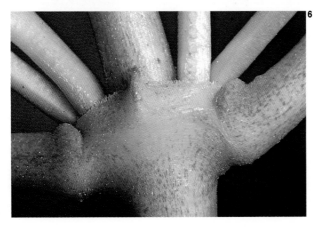

179

Mamangi *Coprosma arborea,* and *Coprosma macrocarpa*

Mamangi is found in forest from North Cape south to Kawhia and Tokomaru Bay. *C. macrocarpa* is found in forest from North Cape to Kaipara Harbour.

Fig 1 Spray of mamangi foliage showing the typical winged petioles of the leaves.

Fig 2 The stipule of mamangi. (x5)

Fig 3 The waxy, leathery, somewhat wavy leaves of *C. macrocarpa*. (x0.5)

Fig 4 *C. macrocarpa* stipule. (x5)

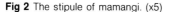

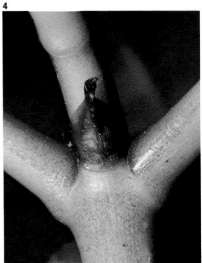

Taupata *Coprosma repens*
and **karamu** *C. robusta*

Taupata is found in coastal areas from North Cape to Marlborough and Greymouth. Karamu is found throughout the North and South Islands in forests and scrublands.

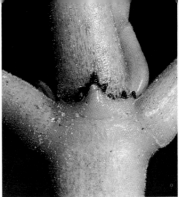

3

1

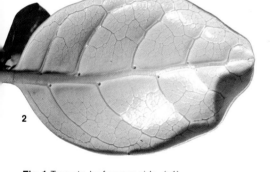

2

4

5

Fig 1 Taupata leaf upper side. (x1)

Fig 2 Taupata leaf underside. (x1)

Fig 3 Taupata stipule. (x3)

Fig 4 Karamu leaf upper side. (x0.5)

Fig 5 Karamu leaf underside. (x0.5)

Fig 6 The stipule of karamu. (x3)

6

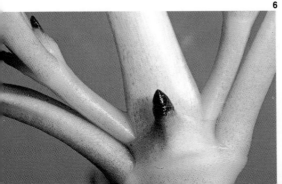

Kanono   *Coprosma grandifolia*

Kanono is found throughout the
North and South Islands in
forests and scrublands.

Fig 1 Leaf upper side. (x0.5)

Fig 2 Leaf underside. (x0.5)

Fig 3 The stipule. (x5)

Fig 4 Kanono trees, with their tall
slender trunks, growing in scrub near
Taupo, 1974.

182

Round-leaved coprosma *Coprosma rotundifolia*
and **thin-leaved coprosma** *C. areolata*

Round-leaved coprosma is found throughout New Zealand from sea level to 600 m, mainly in damp situations and along stream banks. Thin-leaved coprosma is found throughout New Zealand in forest from sea level to 960 m.

1

2

3

4

Fig 1 Upper surface of the small leaves of round-leaved coprosma. (x2)

Fig 2 The stipule of round-leaved coprosma. (x5.5)

Fig 3 Leaf spray of thin-leaved coprosma showing winged petioles, which are hairy.

Fig 4 The hairy stipule of thin-leaved coprosma. (x6)

183

Coprosma crassifolia and **wavy-leaved coprosma** C. tenuifolia

C. crassifolia, with its spreading, interlacing, stiff branches, is found throughout the North and South Islands from sea level to 400 m. Wavy-leaved coprosma is found from Thames south to the Ruahine Ranges, mainly inside forests.

Fig 1 C. crassifolia leaves, upper sides. (x3)

Fig 2 The pale lower surfaces of the thick, leathery leaves of C. crassifolia. (x3)

Fig 3 C. crassifolia drupes are yellowish. (x3)

Fig 4 The stipule and hairy petioles of C. crassifolia. (x9)

Fig 5 The stipule of wavy-leaved coprosma has denticles surrounded by hairs. (x4)

Fig 6 A spray of wavy-leaved coprosma foliage.

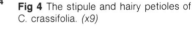

184

Stinkwood/Hupiro *Coprosma foetidissima* and mikimiki/yellow-wood *C. linariifolia*

Stinkwood is found from sea level to 1,360 m in forests from Coromandel south throughout New Zealand. It is easily recognised by the foul smell of rotten eggs emitted whenever it is brushed against, broken or crushed. Mikimiki is found from Thames south to Southland from sea level to 900 m in forest and scrub.

Fig 1 Foliage spray of stinkwood. The leaves have winged petioles and are varied in shape. (x0.5)

Fig 2 Female flowers of stinkwood are solitary and the drupes are sparse. (x2)

Fig 3 Foliage spray of mikimiki showing thick, leathery leaves, 20–30 mm long and the long, tubular sheath of the stipules.

Fig 4 Mikimiki stipules. (x2.5)

Mingimingi *Coprosma propinqua*

Found from Mangonui south throughout New Zealand in swampy forests and scrub, along streams and river banks and in stoney places.

3

1

5

Fig 1 Mingimingi trees, upper Waipunga Valley, 1966.

Fig 2 Mingimingi drupes are blue. (x0.8)

Fig 3 Upper surfaces of the thick, leathery leaves. (x3.5)

Fig 4 Leaf lower surfaces. (x3.5)

Fig 5 The stipule of mingimingi. (x6)

2

Leafy coprosma *Coprosma parviflora* and **stiff karamu** *C. rigida*

Leafy coprosma is found around Kaitaia in scrubland. Stiff karamu has characteristic stiff, spreading, intertwining branches and a reddish bark. It is found from Mangonui southwards throughout New Zealand in forests and along forest margins.

Fig 1 Leafy coprosma leaves occur as fascicles on stiff, spreading branches.

Fig 2 Leaf undersides, hairy stem and petioles of leafy coprosma. (x4)

Fig 3 Leafy coprosma's hairy stipule, petioles and stem. (x7.5)

Fig 4 The red bark and two drupes of stiff karamu, April. (x3)

Fig 5 Stiff karamu branchlets with sparse, thick, leathery leaves 2–3 mm long.

Fig 6 The stipule of stiff karamu. (x7)

The genus *Olearia*

Contains thirty-two species in the New Zealand region, of which nineteen grow as small trees 3–10 m high. Their daisy-like flowers occur as solitary, large flower heads up to 5 cm across with both ray and disc florets; as racemes of flower heads up to 3 cm across with many disc florets; as corymbs of small flower heads with both disc and ray florets; or as corymbs of tiny flower heads each with a single disc floret. Their bark is usually thin and papery, peeling in thin strips or flakes and their branchlets are normally tomentose.

Hakeke/Hakekeke *Olearia ilicifolia*

Found from sea level to 1,200 m, mainly in the mountains, from East Cape to Stewart Island. South Island plants have wider leaves than North Island plants.

Fig 1 Hakeke tree growing in the Hollyford Valley, 1975.

1

Fig 2 Hakeke bark.

Fig 3 Upper surface of a typical hakeke leaf from the South Island showing the grooved petiole. (approx x1)

Fig 4 A grooved branchlet with its soft tomentum. (x4)

Fig 5 Upper surface of a typical hakeke leaf from the North Island. (approx x1)

Fig 6 The lower surfaces of hakeke leaves have a yellowish to ochraceous, satiny tomentum.

Fig 7 Corymbs of hakeke flower heads on their long, stout stalks, December.

Family *Compositae*
Genus *Olearia*

189

Heketara *Olearia rani*

Found throughout the North Island and in Nelson and Marlborough from sea level to 800 m, in forest clearings, along forest margins, along streams and river banks and in scrub.

Fig 1 Spray showing leaf upper surfaces, tomentose branchlets and alternate leaf arrangement.

Fig 2 Panicles of flower heads, November.

Fig 3 Lower surface of a leaf showing dense tomentum and prominent leaf veins. (approx x1)

Coromandel tree daisy *Olearia townsonii* and muttonbird scrub/tete a weka *O. angustifolia*

Coromandel tree daisy is found in rocky places above the Kauaeranga Valley, near Thames. Muttonbird scrub is found in coastal areas of Southland and Stewart Island.

1

Fig 1 A spray of Coromandel tree daisy showing flower heads and leaf upper surfaces.

Fig 2 Lower surface of a Coromandel tree daisy leaf. (approx x1)

Fig 3 The lightly grooved, four-angled branchlet of Coromandel tree daisy with its shining tomentum. (x2)

Fig 4 A spray of muttonbird scrub showing large, scented flowers and the thick, leathery leaves with marginal, calloused teeth and soft tomentum on lower surfaces. (x0.5)

3

4

Olearia thomsonii and **common tree daisy** *O. arborescens*

O. thomsonii is found in the Ohura Basin near Taumarunui and the common tree daisy is found from sea level to 1,200 m in forest and scrub, from the Bay of Plenty south to Stewart Island.

Fig 1 The angular, reddish branchlet of *O. thomsonii.* (x2)

Fig 2 A foliage spray of *O. thomsonii.*

Fig 3 A foliage spray of common tree daisy. (x0.75)

Fig 4 Flowers of common tree daisy showing also the square branchlet and leaf petiole, December. (x1)

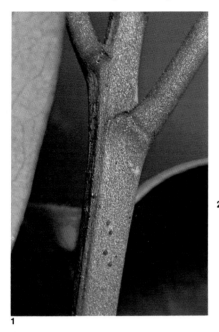

Streamside tree daisy   *Olearia cheesmanii*

Found from Coromandel south to about Westport along streams near forest margins.

Fig 1 Streamside tree daisy in full flower, October.

Fig 2 The lower surface of a leaf. (x1)

Fig 3 The grooved, tomentose branchlet and a petiole. (x2)

Tanguru   *Olearia albida*

Found in coastal forest from North Cape south to about Tokomaru Bay.

Fig 1 Leaves and flower heads of tanguru, April.

Fig 2 The lower surface of a leaf, showing tomentum and veins. (approx x1)

Fig 3 A grooved branchlet with its dense, fluffy tomentum which also covers the petiole and a new bud. (x3.5)

194

Thick-leaved tree daisy *Olearia pachyphylla*

Found usually in scrub throughout coastal areas of the Bay of Plenty.

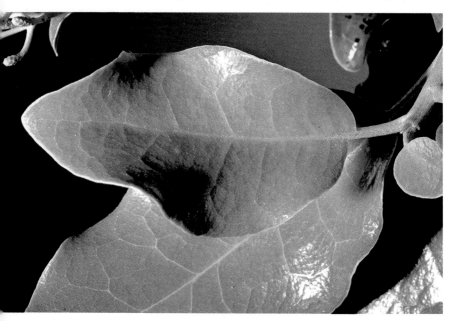

Fig 1 Upper surface of the glossy, thick, leathery leaves, showing also the stout, pubescent petiole. (x1)

Fig 2 The leaf lower surface with its tomentum and raised midvein. (x1)

Akepiro/Tanguru   *Olearia furfuracea*

Found from sea level to 600 m along forest margins and streams
and in scrub from North Cape to the Southern Ruahine range.

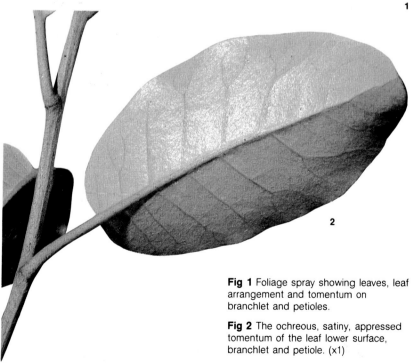

Fig 1 Foliage spray showing leaves, leaf
arrangement and tomentum on
branchlet and petioles.

Fig 2 The ochreous, satiny, appressed
tomentum of the leaf lower surface,
branchlet and petiole. (x1)

Rough-leaved tree daisy *Olearia lacunosa*

The rough-leaved tree daisy is found in mountain forests and scrub between 600–900 m altitude, from the Tararua Range south to about Franz Josef Glacier.

1

Fig 1 A spray of foliage showing both upper and lower surfaces of the thick, leathery leaves.

Fig 2 The trees often have twisted and gnarled branches; *O. lacunosa* trees beside a sinkhole on Mt Arthur, Nelson, 1973.

2

Akeake   *Olearia avicenniaefolia*

Found from sea level to 900 m in scrubland throughout the South and Stewart Islands.

1   2

3

Fig 1 Upper surface of a leaf, showing the grooved petiole. (x0.75)

Fig 2 Leaf underside showing the appressed tomentum and the distinct venation. (x0.75)

Fig 3 The light-coloured, thin, papery bark, peeling in strips.

198

Akiraho *Olearia paniculata* and **coastal tree daisy** *O. solandri*

Akiraho is found along forest margins and in scrub from East Cape and Raglan south to about Oamaru and Greymouth. Coastal tree daisy occurs in coastal areas from North Cape south to the Clarence River and Westport.

Fig 1 A foliage spray of akiraho showing the white tomentum on the leaf lower surfaces.

Fig 3 Corymbs of many small akiraho flower heads, March.

Fig 2 The angled, tomentose akiraho branchlet with a petiole. (x4.5)

Fig 4 A typical spray of coastal tree daisy with flowers, April.

Fragrant tree daisy   *Olearia fragrantissima*

Found in scrub and along forest margins from Banks Peninsula south. It has stiff, zigzagging branches and a strong scent reminiscent of peaches.

Fig 1 A foliage spray showing leaves and flower clusters.

Fig 2 The underside of fragrant tree daisy leaves showing the soft, white tomentum. (x1)

Fig 3 Fragrant tree daisy flower heads form dense clusters up to 2 cm across. (x2)

Deciduous tree daisy *Olearia hectori*

Found in scrubland from sea level to 900 m around Taihape and from the Clarence River to Southland. It has smooth, rounded branchlets and is deciduous.

Fig 1 Foliage spray showing how the leaves vary in shape and occur in opposite fascicles of two to four.

Fig 2 A branchlet with an opposite pair of arrested branchlets bearing leaves and showing their undersides. (x1)

Fig 3 Flower heads, September. (x4)

Twiggy tree daisy *Olearia virgata*

Found from sea level to 1,050 m in scrub and boggy ground from Thames south to Stewart Island. The slender branches divaricate and are hairy only when young.

Fig 1 Leaf upper surfaces; these occur in widely separated opposite fascicles of two to four each. (x2.5)

Fig 2 Leaf undersides, showing thick tomentum. (x2.5)

Fig 3 Flower heads, November. (x4)

Brown-backs
Brachyglottis elaeagnifolia
and B. rotundifolia

B. elaeagnifolia is found
between about 800 and 950 m
altitude in the North Island south
from Te Aroha Mountain. *B.
rotundifolia* is found in coastal
areas of the South Island south
of Jackson Bay and on Stewart
Island.

Fig 1 *B. elaeagnifolia* spray with leaves
and a flower head on its woolly
branchlet.

Fig 2 The thick,
leathery leaves and
tomentum of *B.
elaeagnifolia*. The
leaves are 6–9 cm
long by 3–5 cm
wide.

Fig 3 Leaves of *B.
rotundifolia* showing
the 5 cm-long
grooved petioles.
The leaves are 4–10
cm long by 4–9 cm
wide.

Family *Compositae*
Genus *Brachyglottis*

Rangiora *Brachyglottis repanda*

A small tree up to 7 m high, found from North Cape south to Kaikoura and Greymouth in forest, along forest margins and in scrub, from sea level to 750 m.

Fig 1 Lower surface of a rangiora leaf showing white tomentum and raised veins. (x0.5) The leaf varies from 5–25 cm long and 5–20 cm wide with a stout, grooved petiole up to 10 cm long.

Fig 2 A rangiora tree in full flower showing the leaf upper surfaces, September.

204

Kohuhurangi   *Brachyglottis hectori*

Found in the South Island only, between 100 and 1,050 m altitude along streams and forest margins from Nelson south to Greymouth.

1

2   3

Fig 1 Kohuhurangi in flower, Takaka Hill, January 1972.

Fig 2 Upper surfaces of the leaves which occur around the tips of the

branchlets. The leaves are soft and 10–25 cm long by 4–12 cm wide.

Fig 3 The daisy-like flower, January. (x1)

Kohurangi *Urostemon kirkii*

Found from sea level to 780 m in forest throughout the North Island. It may grow as an epiphyte or ground shrub but in the north it grows as a small tree.

1 2

Fig 1 A tree of var. *angustior* growing in Waipoua Forest, 1970. This variety is found around Auckland and in Northland.

Fig 2 Upper surfaces of kohurangi leaves. (x1.5)

Fig 3 Upper surfaces of leaves of

var. *angustior.* (x0.5) These leaves vary between 5–12 cm long by 1–2 cm wide. (x0.5)

Fig 4 Flowers of kohurangi occur as corymbs. (x1)

Family *Compositae*
Genus *Brachyglottis*

3 4

Koromiko-taranga   *Hebe parviflora*   var.   *arborea*

A small tree up to
7.5 m high, found in
coastal areas from
Whangarei south to
Marlborough and in
the central North
Island high country.

Fig 1 A grove of trees on
the Rimutaka Hill, 1966.

Fig 2 A raceme of flowers,
February. (x2)

Fig 3 A spray showing the
long, narrow leaves, each
2.5–7 cm long and about
4 mm wide.

Family *Scrophulariaceae*
Genus *Hebe*

207

Poroporo *Solanum aviculare* and *S. laciniatum*

Small trees or shrubs up to 3 m high with soft, shining green, membraneous leaves up to 40 cm long. *S. laciniatum* always has purplish-coloured stems while *S. aviculare* has greenish stems. Both species are found in scrub and along coastal and lowland forest margins. *S. laciniatum* occurs from Auckland south to Dunedin and *S. aviculare* south to Banks Peninsula in the east and Karamea in the west.

Fig 1 Flowers of *S. laciniatum,* October (x1) Flowers of *S. aviculare* are smaller and lavender or white in colour.

Fig 2 Leaves of *S. laciniatum,* upper surfaces.

Fig 3 Berries of *S. aviculare,* April. (x0.6)

Family *Solanaceae*
Genus *Solanum*

Ngaio *Myoporum laetum*

A tree up to 10 m high with a trunk up to 30 cm through. In exposed places it is often dome-shaped. Found throughout the North Island and in the South Island south to Otago.

Fig 1 A foliage spray showing the alternating, fleshy, gland-dotted leaves on their flattened petioles. (x0.6)

Fig 3 A dome-shaped ngaio on the Kaikoura Coast, 1964.

Fig 2 The axillary flowers arise in clusters of 2–6 and each flower is 1–1.5 cm across, December. (x0.6)

Family *Myoporaceae*
Genus *Myoporum*

Puriri   *Vitex lucens*

A massive tree up to 20 m high with stout, spreading branches and a trunk up to 1.5 m through. Found in coastal and lowland forests in Northland and the northern part of the Coromandel Peninsula.

1

2

Fig 1 A fine puriri tree on the Coromandel Peninsula, 1966.

Fig 2 Clusters of puriri flowers. The trees flower during most of the year.

Fig 3 Upper surface of the distinctive compound puriri leaf. The upper three leaflets are 5–12.5 cm long and 3–5 cm wide and the petiole is 3.5–12.5 cm long.

Fig 4 Ripening puriri drupes, February. (x0.5)

Family *Verbenaceae*
Genus *Vitex*

Mangrove/manawa *Avicennia marina* var. *resinifera*

A small tree which grows in tidal waters and may reach 15 m high. It is found from North Cape south to Kawhia Harbour in the west and Ohiwa Harbour in the east. Only in the far north does it grow taller than a few metres.

1   3

4

Fig 1 A tall manawa tree in an estua near Paihia, 1965.

Fig 2 A spray of the thick, leathery manawa leaves. Each leaf is 5–10 cm long by 2–4 cm wide.

Fig 3 A flower bud and a flower, Apr (x5)

Fig 4 Manawa fruit capsules, Decem (x0.25)

212

5

6

Fig 5 A manawa tree
at low tide in
Tapotupotu Bay,
showing the aerial
roots coming up
through the mud.
Cape Reinga, 1970.

Fig 6 Aerial roots of
a manawa tree.

Family *Avicenniaceae*
Genus *Avicennia*

Cabbage trees: genus *Cordyline*

A feature of the New Zealand landscape, being found along the edges of forests and swamps, along river banks, or standing alone and in groups in fields and on hillsides.

Ti kouka/Cabbage tree *Cordyline australis*

Found throughout the country, from sea level to 600 m, this tree reaches a height of 20 m. The flowers are strongly sweet-scented.

Fig 1 A very old ti kouka in full flower, Hinakura, November 1970.

Fig 2 A close view of some flowers from a panicle which can reach 1.5 m long, December. (x2)

Family *Agavaceae*
Genus *Cordyline*

Ti ngahere/Ti parae/Forest cabbage tree *Cordyline banskii*

Ti ngahere grows to about 4 m high, usually with several stems which arise near the ground. The flower panicle, 1–2 m long, is more openly branched than that of ti kouka.

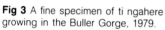
3 4

Fig 3 A fine specimen of ti ngahere growing in the Buller Gorge, 1979.

Fig 4 A section of a ti ngahere flower panicle, November.

Toii/Broad-leaved or mountain cabbage tree   *Cordyline indivisa*

Toii grows to 8 m high with a massive trunk and is found from the Hunua Ranges south to Fiordland, particularly in the wetter areas, from 450 to 1,350 m altitude in open parts of forests where there is plenty of light.

Fig 5 A flower panicle of toii hanging below the leafy crown, December.

Fig 6 A fine specimen of toii growing on Mt Egmont, 1965.

5 6

215

A palm tree reaching to 10 m in height, found throughout the North Island in lowland forests and in the South Island south to Banks Peninsula in the east and Greymouth in the west.

Fig 1 A nikau palm growing in the pure nikau stand at Morere Springs, 1977.

Fig 2 The inflorescence bears both male and female flowers arranged in threes; this photo shows a small female flower bud sandwiched between two male flower buds and an open male flower, December. (x3)

Fig 3 An inflorescence of the present season on top, with inflorescences of the previous season below now bearing fruits, February.

Fig 4 An inflorescence a short while after opening, February.

Fig 5 A flower spike in bud with flowers starting to open, and a fruiting spike from the previous year now fully ripe, February.

Family *Palmae*
Genus *Rhopalostylis*

Glossary

acuminate: tapering to a fine point

alternate: arising singly along an axis

appressed: closely and flatly pressed against a surface

ascending: growing upwards, usually at a narrow angle from the vertical

attenuate: gradually tapering to an apex

axil: the upper angle between two dissimilar parts

berry: a fleshy fruit containing a number of seeds but not a "stone"

capitulum: the flower-head of Compositae

capsule: a dry fruit that splits open to release its seeds

carpel: the female unit of a flower consisting of the ovary, style and stigma

compound: formed of several similar parts

compressed: flattened

cone: the fruiting parts of a conifer

corymb: a more or less flat-topped raceme

crenate: with shallow, rounded teeth

crenulate: with very small shallow, rounded teeth

cupule: a cup-shaped structure

cyme: an inflorescence, usually symmetrical, with the oldest flowers innermost

dentate: with sharp teeth at right angles to the margin

denticle: a very small tooth

denticulate: with very small teeth along the margin

disk: the central mass of fertile florets in the capitulum of Compositae

divaricating: intertangled stems spreading at a wide angle

domatia: small pits on the lower surface of a leaf or between the mid and lateral veins

drupe: a fruit with a "stone" or seed surrounded by a fleshy layer

emarginate: with a shallow notch at the apex

fascicled: with a close or tight bundle or cluster

foliate: leaved

foliolate: bearing leaflets

frond: a leaf, especially of ferns

fruit: the ripened ovary containing the seeds

inflorescence: a general term for the flowering parts

leaflet: one element of a compound leaf

nut: an indehiscent, single-seeded fruit with woody surrounding layer

opposite: (of leaves) with a pair arising at the same level on opposite sides of the stem

panicle: branched indeterminate inflorescence

pedicel: the stalk of an individual flower

phylloclade: a flattened stem which functions as a leaf

pinnate: compound with the parts arranged on either side of the axis

pubescent: clad in short, soft hairs

pungent: ending in a sharp, stiff point

raceme: an unbranched indeterminate inflorescence

ray-florets: the outer ring of florets in the capitulum of Compositae

rhachis (rachis): the axis of an inflorescence or of a compound leaf

serrate: sharply toothed

serrulate: with very small, sharp teeth

sessile: without any stalk

spike: an unbranched, indeterminate, elongate inflorescence with sessile flowers

staminode: a stamen that has no pollen, usually without an anther

stipule: a scale-like or leaf-like appendage at the base of a leaf petiole; usually in pairs

stoma: a pore in the leaf epidermis through which gases pass

tomentose: having a covering of soft, matted, appressed hairs

tomentum: a dense covering of more or less matted, appressed, soft hairs

trifoliate: having three leaves

trifoliolate: having three leaflets

umbel: a more or less umbrella-shaped inflorescence with its pedicels arising from a common centre

vein: a strand of conducting and usually strengthening tissue in a leaf

venation: the arrangement of the veins in a leaf

whorl: an arrangement of three or more parts at the same level around an axis

Index of common names

This special index contains the common names of the New Zealand tree species.

General index

The names in bold italic are those of the native tree species
featured in this book.